NEW TESTAMENT
EVERYDAY BIBLE STUDIES

NEW TESTAMENT
EVERYDAY BIBLE STUDIES

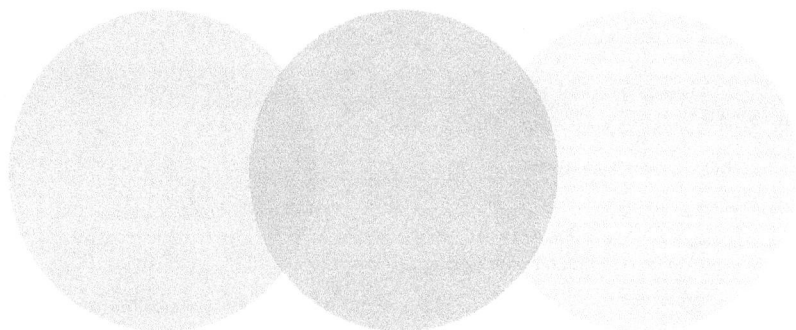

1, 2, 3 JOHN

LIVING A LIFE IN LIGHT AND LOVE

SCOT MCKNIGHT

QUESTIONS WRITTEN BY
BECKY CASTLE MILLER

HarperChristian
Resources

New Testament Everyday Bible Study Series: 1–3 John

© 2025 by Scot McKnight

Published by HarperChristian Resources, 3950 Sparks Drive SE, Suite 101, Grand Rapids, MI 49546, USA. HarperChristian Resources is a registered trademark of HarperCollins Christian Publishing, Inc.

Requests for information should be addressed to customercare@harpercollins.com.

ISBN 978-0-310-12959-2 (softcover)
ISBN 978-0-310-12960-8 (ebook)

HarperCollins Publishers, Macken House, 39/40 Mayor Street Upper, Dublin 1, D01 C9W8, Ireland (https://www.harpercollins.com)

First Printing May 2025

CONTENTS

2 JOHN

3 JOHN

To the Doctor of Ministry Students
Houston Theological Seminary

GENERAL INTRODUCTION

C hristians make a claim for the Bible not made of any other book. Or, since the Bible is a library shelf of many authors, it's a claim we make of no other shelf of books. We claim that God worked in each of the authors as they were writing so that what was scratched on papyrus expressed what God wanted communicated to the people of God. Which makes the New Testament (NT) a book unlike any other book. Which is why Christians are reading the NT almost two thousand years later with great delight. These books have the power to instruct us and to rebuke us and to correct us and to train us to walk with God every day. We read these books because God speaks to us in them.

Developing a routine of reading the Bible with an open heart, a receptive mind, and a flexible will is the why of the *New Testament Everyday Bible Studies*. But not every day will be the same. Some days we pause and take it in and other days we stop and repent and lament and open ourselves to God's restoring graces. No one word suffices for what the

Bible does to us. In fact, the Bible's view of the Bible can be found by reading Psalm 119, the longest chapter in the Bible with 176 verses! It is a meditation on eight terms for what the Bible is and what the Bible does to those who listen and read it. Its laws instruct us and order us, its statutes direct us, its precepts inform us, its decrees guide us, its commands compel us, its words speak to us, and its promises comfort us, and it is no wonder that the author can sum all eight up as the "way" (119:3). Each of those terms still speaks to what happens when we open our minds to the Word of God.

Every day with the Bible then is new because our timeless and timely God communes with us in our daily lives in our world and in our time. Just as God spoke to Jesus in Galilee and Paul in Ephesus and John on Patmos. These various contexts help us hear God in our context, so the *New Testament Everyday Bible Studies* will often delve into contexts. Most of us now have a Bible on our devices. We may well have several translations available to us everywhere we go every day. To hear those words, we are summoned by God to open the Bible, to attune our hearts to God, and to listen to what God says. My prayer is that these daily study guides will help each of us become daily Bible readers attentive to the mind of God.

INTRODUCTION: READING THE EXHORTATIONS OF JOHN

One ought not read John's exhortations the way one reads Paul's. It won't work. Analyzing John's exhortations the way we break down the arguments in Romans or Galatians dismantles John's exhortations. The prose of 1 John is an aesthetic. Short sentences, repeating vocabulary, simple ideas—each arises both gently and obtrusively. Soon we are snagged in his web. The same word appears again. Nothing of John's theology surprises. The shortness and the repetition, however, deepen his ideas until we admit he's taken us in. Before long we feel we are overcome with the glories of life, light, and love—three short words in English and in Greek: *zoē, phōs, agapē*. He adds to these truth, commands, and obedience. They're as connected to one another as uncles, cousins, second cousins, and cousins twice removed.

The apostle Paul wrote quickly and often. He revised. His

friends advised him to cut and shorten and explain himself. He edited and rewrote. John endured the silence of waiting for the right word to appear. John writes out of silence, Paul in the din and bustle of the noisy traffic of Ephesus. Neither of the authors doubts that the center of one true life is to be found only in Jesus Christ. But they approach living for Jesus differently. The big ideas of each flow from the life of each, and because of that, their letters vibrate and resonate with life as it is. But John's style exceeds the literary, exceeds what one expects from a letter. His prose, his style expresses and elicits a spirituality. A spirituality that utters wisdom when it has something to say, but not until then. Paul discovered what he had to say by thinking, talking, arguing, writing. John waited, seemingly alone, in silence until the word arrived. He flipped over his three favorite terms to discover what was under each. Together they speak to one another and, combined, to us. Differently, but to us anyway. John's secrets are not discovered until we read him slowly.

John's so-called first letter, though not actually a letter as 2 and 3 John are, reveals an authentic pastoral voice. It could be a sermon, a homily, or an address, but it was written out and sent, or at least given, to believers. I will call it an "exhortation." The believers are in John's circle of ministry. He routinely uses "we" and "ours" and "us." We could easily think this exhortation was sent to the seven churches in Revelation 2–3. His exhortation is not an argument, not a logical flow with a premise, a problem, and proposals proven by evidence. John loves these people. His exhortation sounds at times like a sermon, at other times like a private conversation, at times like a theological statement, and at all times like a heart bleeding God's life, light, and love. His heart could not have written any other kind of exhortation. His repetitions are not calculated; they express what matters most to him.

John's exhortation mirrors his heart's reflections. He follows no rules for writing. Rules cannot capture how he writes. If rules for reflection could be written, they would be formed out of John's reflections. Good writers shape what is written for a specific audience. The prose of John is like a Celtic knot that loops back and goes under and over itself until what you see is the whole knot each time you look at one part (see the front cover of this book for an example). John knew his audience needed this kind of message from himself.

One feature of his audience was some people denying that Jesus had come in the flesh—a divinity whose feet didn't touch the ground. They may have argued Jesus only seemed to be a human but really wasn't. This group, often called "secessionists," split from the churches to whom John writes these letters. You can read about them in 1 John 2:22; 4:2–3; 5:12–13, and that they seceded from the mother church is seen in 2:19. Third John names someone who may have been a leader among the secessionists (Diotrephes). Anger would be a common response to those who have left the community. Or perhaps relief, perhaps tinged with doubt about whether or not those who remained were in the right. John assures them they are. He knows whereof he speaks. Judith Lieu gets it exactly right when she writes, "The author of 1 John lives in a thought-world of confident assertions and clear certainties" (Lieu, *1–3 John,* 67).

Second John is written to (evidently) a woman leader of the early church, probably in a church in John's circle of churches (Smyrna, Pergamum, Thyatira, Sardis, Philadelphia, or Laodicea), and 3 John is sent to Gaius, who is also probably in one of these churches. Many suggest these three books were written in the last quarter of the first century AD, and those who connect the letters to John—and we will clarify that name immediately below—think the setting is Ephesus. A very helpful guide to Ephesus, one of the world's great cities of the time, is by Sandra Glahn. The city flourished in business, hosted an intellectual culture, and led in the religious worship of the protector goddess, Artemis, as well as a growing cult to the emperor (Glahn, *Ephesus*, 3–9, 29–32). The Christian community would have been challenged daily by the idolatries and the worship of Artemis. Ephesus, in fact, experienced the diversity of earliest Christianity: Paul centered his Aegean mission in Ephesus; Mary, mother of Jesus, may have resided in Ephesus; Priscilla and Aquila as well as Timothy resided for a time in Ephesus; variants of the faith arose here. Paul's first letter to the Corinthians as well as Ephesians and 1 and 2 Timothy arose from Ephesus. Which leads to the Gospel of John and 1, 2, and 3 John as yet more texts deriving from Ephesus. The book of Revelation, written from the island of Patmos, was first sent to Ephesus (Revelation 2:1–7). Before the church was centered in Rome, it was centered in Ephesus.

A word about authorship. The "elder" writes both 2 and 3 John. No attribution is given for 1 John. We can work from the two shorter letters back to 1 John. The vocabulary and style of 2 John evokes 1 John so clearly one has to think they are by the same author, as the church's tradition has always had it. However, the "John" here could be either the apostle John or a slightly younger Elder John. In the second century AD, Papias (quoted later by Eusebius) distinguished the Elder John from the apostle John. Here are his words:

> . . . but if someone came who had followed the elders, I made inquiry about the words of the elders, what Andrew or Peter said, or what Philip or what Thomas or James, or what John or Matthias or any other of the Lord's disciples, or what Aristion and the presbyter [elder] John, disciples of the Lord, said." (Eusebius, *Ecclesiastical History* 3.39.4; translation by Schott)

In case you wonder if Papias wasn't clear about whether the presbyter/Elder John was the apostle John, Eusebius clarifies the words, writing,

> Here it is worth recognizing that he counts the name of John twice. The first time he catalogues him with Peter, James, Matthias, and the rest of the apostles, clearly meaning the evangelist [apostle John who wrote the Gospel of John], but by using a distinctive phrase he ranks the other [elder] John with the others outside the number of the apostles, ranking Aristion before him, and clearly naming him a presbyter. This proves the truth of the account of there being two homonymous men in Asia and two tombs in Ephesus, each of which is still said to be John's. And

one must apply one's intellect to this. For it is likely that the second John (unless one wishes to claim the first) witnessed the Apocalypse that bears the name of John. The Papias we are now discussing confesses that he received the words of the apostles from those who followed them, but he says that he heard Aristion and the presbyter John with his own ears. (Eusebius, *Ecclesiastical History* 3.39.5; translation by Schott)

There were two Johns in Ephesus. One was the apostle, one was the elder. The apostle was older than the "elder" John. But is the "elder" of 1, 2 and 3 John the elder alongside Aristion, the one whom Papias himself heard, or is this "elder" the apostle John who wrote the Gospel and 1 John and, for many, the book of Revelation? It is not hard for us to read 2 John and connect it to the author of 1 John. Then we read 1 John and connect it very easily to the Gospel of John. When we proceed like this, we tie all these Johannine books (Gospel, 1–3 John, and Revelation as well) to one and the same author, the apostle John. However, what clouds the tradition is that 2 and 3 John clearly identify the author as the *Elder*, while 1 John does not. The style of these three letters is so similar we need to think of them as written by the same author. He calls himself the Elder. Is it perhaps the case that the Elder identified himself to distinguish himself from the older apostle? Perhaps so. If so, and if the apostle wrote the Gospel of John, the Elder had learned the vocabulary and style of the apostle. An alternative is just as reasonable: the Elder wrote all the Johannine books (Wright and Bird, *The New Testament in Its World*, 652–660, 786–787).

What 1 John asks of us is to sit with him and to listen. To sit alone. With his exhortation. If you are truly alone. If you are genuinely listening to this exhortation's sounds, words, sentences, and ideas, I don't think you can read the short exhortation even in an hour. Don't rush. Please sit there, listening to the tones and timbre and tautness of this man's reflections on life, light, and love. First John has the power to permeate your personality, and if you listen well your vocabulary may change, too.

FOR FURTHER READING

Eusebius, *Ecclesiastical History: A New Translation*, trans. Jeremy M. Schott (Berkeley: University of California, 2019).
N. T. Wright, Michael Bird, *The New Testament in Its World: An Introduction to the History, Literature, and Theology of the First Christians* (Grand Rapids: Zondervan Academic, 2019).

WORKS CITED IN THE STUDY GUIDE

(Throughout this guide you will find the author's name and title in brackets, as noted in this book listing, with page numbers whenever I cite something from it):

Thomas Andrew Bennett, *1–3 John*, The Two Horizons New Testament Commentary (Grand Rapids: Wm. B. Eerdmans, 2021). [Bennett, *1–3 John*]

Constantine R. Campbell, *1, 2, & 3 John*, Story of God Bible Commentary (Grand Rapids: Zondervan, 2017). [Campbell, *1–3 John*]

Miguel G. Echevarría, "Letters of John," in eds. E. McCaulley, Janette H. Ok, Osvaldo Padilla, Amy Peeler, *The New Testament in Color: A Multiethnic Bible Commentary* (Downers Grove: IVP Academic, 2024), 706–727. [Echevarría, "Letters"]

Sandra L. Glahn, *The City of Ephesus: A Short History* (Middletown, Rhode Island: Stone Tower Press, 2024). [Glahn, *Ephesus*]

Karen H. Jobes, *1, 2, & 3 John* (Zondervan Exegetical Commentary on the New Testament; Grand Rapids: Zondervan, 2014). [Jobes, *1–3 John*]

Judith M. Lieu, *I, II, & III John: A Commentary*,
New Testament Library (Louisville:
Westminster John Knox, 2008). [Lieu, *1–3
John*]

Scot McKnight, *The Second Testament: A New
Translation* (Downers Grove: IVP Academic,
2023. [McKnight, *Second Testament*]

Thomas B. Slater, "1–3 John," in B.K. Blount,
Gay L. Byron, Emerson B. Powery, *True
to Our Native Land: An African American
New Testament Commentary*, 2d edition
(Minneapolis: Fortress, 2024), 525–548.
[Slater, "1–3 John"]

1 JOHN

SENSING THE WORD OF LIFE

1 John 1:1–4

(reformatted)

[1] That which was from the beginning,
which we have heard,
which we have seen with our eyes,
which we have looked at and our hands have touched
—this we proclaim concerning the Word of life.
[2] The life appeared;
we have seen it
and testify to it,
and we proclaim to you the eternal life,
which was with the Father and has appeared to us.
[3] We proclaim to you what we have seen and heard,
so that you also may have fellowship with us.
And our fellowship is with the Father and with his Son,
*   Jesus Christ.*
[4] We write this to make our [or, your] joy complete.

The sensory dimension jumps out from today's reading. John's (shared) experience takes us by surprise. He knows Jesus *on the basis of sensory, embodied realities.* He gives special attention to ears and eyes and fingers, to hearing, seeing, and touching (or, better yet, feeling with one's hands; *Second Testament* has "our hands felt" at 1:1; see Luke 24:39; John 20:25–29). John knows Jesus because of his senses. But it's not just John. He uses "we" and "us" and "our" throughout. There is something profoundly sensory about knowing the opening "that which," and the "that which" is Jesus (Campbell, *1–3 John*, 22–23). Mothers *know* the little person who took shape in their wombs by holding them, kissing them, nursing them, touching the head, the face, the ears, the fingers, the tummy, the legs, the toes. The little person *knows* their mother by the same sensory experiences. By the time moms and newborns arrive in the home, the mother knows every inch of that baby. What the mother knows through her eyes is transcended by touch, by kissing, by hugging, by nursing, by holding closely. A healthy mother-child knowing forms through the senses. In fact, that sensory knowing began well before the birth.

So, John knew Jesus. He was, if the tradition is right, the one who rested on the breast of Jesus. Or, as the NIV less sensorily (and more discreetly) translates, "One of them, the disciple whom Jesus loved, was reclining next to him" (John 13:23). In chapter one the NIV gets more sensate, and less discreet, with the same term, translating that the Son was "in closest relationship with the Father" (1:18). What we have in these passages, even more or less discreet translation, can only be named as a sensory, embodied relationship of persons expressing intimacy with one another. This is not embarrassing. Sensory relations between two men are affirmed. John knew Jesus through his senses. He saw Jesus; he heard Jesus; but even more he touched him. As Fleming Rutledge reminds us, "We really cannot separate a person from his body" (Rutledge, *The Bible and* The New York Times, 145). If we cannot separate a person from the body, knowing the person means knowing the body. John surely didn't separate knowing Jesus from knowing the body of Jesus.

The Jesus John sensed was "from the beginning," but just which beginning is not clear. Perhaps creation, or the genesis of the Jesus movement, or the origin of one's personal faith in this Jesus. The Word (Logos) of Life was with the Father and was sent by the Father to the earth, and thus the Word of Life "appeared" to those who sensed him (1:2). John witnessed to and "proclaimed" the Jesus he had sensed (1:1, 3). The word "testify" in 1:2 describes verbal reports about what one has sensed. That is, what one has seen, heard, or observed. Miguel Echevarría is right when he observes that "many Westerners tend to be critical of testimony. They want to see and touch things for themselves, lest they refuse to believe. This is typical of a scientific worldview. For my Cuban family, however, the testimony of our elders was not questioned. . . . What they saw and experienced gave them credibility. So, when our elders spoke, we listened. I believe John expects the same posture from his readers" (Echevarría, "Letters," 709).

Another term that matters in John's exhortation is knowing. He uses the verb "to know" more than twenty times (see

2:13–14). Knowing is more than cognition. Sensate knowing fills out what John even means by knowing. Chemicals are fired up in the kind of knowing John describes in our passage. Each of a person's senses was engaged to know Jesus. Many of us like artworks about Jesus because art depicts the physical, the sensory. I know I like "this" about one image and "that" about another. I resonate with what I know of Jesus. Music adds depth to the painting because it is sensory, and once again the sensory world lights up as we listen to music about Jesus. John's opening poetic lines were music to the ears of those who first heard those words read aloud. As sensory-sensitive listeners, they caught the cadence and were moved by his use of the sounds: *k*'s and *o*'s and *ph*'s and *th*'s. The short lines, each pregnant and ready to give birth to living realities, deepened their own memories of sensory knowing. No wonder we are left wondering if the joy was John's or theirs in verse four.* The joy about which John writes is what Jesus prayed for (John 16:20–24; 17:13).

Back to the mother and child. A child knows love by touch, by proximity, by the senses. The child experiences cognition, however undeveloped, in the love and warmth through the senses experienced in the mother's embrace. Sensory knowing comes first. John knew Jesus first through the sensory. John's terms like light and life probe what he had learned by his senses.

---

* *The Greek term for "our" is* hēmōn *and the Greek term for "your" is* humōn. *Both were pronounced "hee-mown." Because those who copied manuscripts were read to by someone, and since these both sound the same, some manuscripts have the former and others the latter.*

SENSING JESUS

John, who loves the first-person words "we" and "our" and "us" (used some fifteen times in today's reading), joined others in witnessing something far greater than Ephesus, which was the third-largest city in the world at the time. Far greater than Artemis, who was worshiped in one of the architectural wonders of the world at the time. That temple to Artemis was plundered by the Goths and burned about two centuries after John wrote this exhortation. John, suggesting he's not the only one with this (shared) sensory experience of Jesus, has "heard" and "seen" and "looked at" and "touched" none other than "the Word of Life," that is Jesus Christ, God incarnate, the One who was "from the beginning" of all creation. John was there. He touched Jesus, and Jesus touched him. He heard Jesus. He saw Jesus. The foundation of this exhortation is that John was a witness. Of course, he seems to broaden his own witness to include others, who could be the ones who make up his "we" and "us" and "ours." Perhaps you might be wondering if John's "we" is a polite way of saying "I." That "*we* write" becomes "*I* write" many times suggests so (2:1, 7, 8, 12, 13, 14, 21, 26; 5:13). Though at the time of this exhortation he resided in Ephesus, he had witnessed Jesus in his earthly life. John grew up and was nurtured in Judaism on the northern tip of the Sea of Galilee. He encountered Jesus on the shore when Jesus summoned him and his brother to drop their nets so they could follow him. He observed Jesus preaching, teaching, debating, healing, caring for, and doing mighty miracles. He entered Jerusalem with Jesus and left without Jesus. He experienced the crucifixion and the resurrection. Because he was a witness, John proclaims and testifies about Jesus to believers in Ephesus. Yet, at some level, this is not John's experience alone. John's "we" requires that we find our experience in John's shared experience with other witnesses to Jesus, some of whom, like us, had not touched Jesus as John himself had.

Some were denying what John knew was true: Jesus is Israel's long-expected Messiah (2:22); Jesus is God come-in-the-flesh (4:2); and Jesus is the one true source of life (5:11–13). In today's reading, John says "we proclaim . . . eternal life," which means Jesus is *himself* that eternal life (Slater, "1–3 John," 530–531). He is not only Eternal Life itself, he ushers in the Life that is eternal. (These words echo words in John 1:1–18.) John's crisp, poetic language quickly forms into a warning to those who are walking away with bad ideas (2:19). John was a witness to a real human who was the Messiah and who was God incarnate. He knows because he sensed him. His memory allows him to sense him a generation or two after Jesus' death and resurrection. John writes for those who affirm what he proclaims as a witness.

SENSING JESUS TODAY

Those who affirm these truths about Jesus participate in a common life (*Second Testament*), which the NIV translates as "fellowship" (1:3). Fellowship with one another unites persons in a common sharing of life "with the Father and with his Son, Jesus Christ" (1:3). Fellowship, too, is a sensory term.

We know one another through our senses, just as John knew Jesus. The only way we know one another is through our senses. The more senses involved, the deeper our knowledge. But our common life shares in the divine. As Thomas Bennett writes, "Whether we live in the first generation after Jesus's life and ministry or the present day, this notion that we truly share God's character should strike us as utterly scandalous, for the relations holding between the Father and Son are endlessly mutual" (Bennett, *1–3 John*, 17). Think about it: we are sharing the common life shared between Father, Son, and I add Spirit.

Those who talk meaningfully about Jesus are witnesses to their experience of Jesus. We learn to know Jesus in three ways:

In the reading about him in the New Testament,
in learning of him through one another,
and in our personal communion with him.

One of my pastor friends asks those he knows this simple question: What is Jesus teaching you today? But some miss this kind of sensory knowing because they turn Jesus into a set of ideas. I sometimes put a theology book down or move away from a Christian media site I'm reading. Too often they reduce Jesus to his role (Messiah, Savior, Lord) and erase that he was a person. I say to myself, *Where's Jesus in what these folks are writing?* In this study guide I will keep the person and personality of Jesus in front of us by returning to the Gospel of John. Bodies matter. Fleming Rutledge writes,

"The ultimate proof that bodies matter is that Jesus had one" (Rutledge, *The Bible and* The New York Times, 149). There we encounter the man from Galilee, the one John witnessed. Concentrating too much on ideas about Jesus, theology called Christology, doctrinal propositions about Jesus, or some role or title of Jesus has the power to erase Jesus as a real, living person. If there's anything John cares about it, it is the One he saw and heard and touched. What he believed about Jesus flowed from his sensory experience of Jesus.

John witnessed the Jesus who interacted with John the Baptist when the Baptist was interrogated by Jewish leaders about who he thought he was. He told them he was not the Messiah. Instead, he was the "voice" who was given one mission from God: to speak about Jesus. The Baptist was unworthy of being that witness (John 1:19–28). So sensory-overloading and supreme and superior was Jesus to the Baptist that the Baptist confessed, when he witnessed Jesus himself, that Jesus was the Lamb of God who gained victory over sins. The Baptist saw the Spirit descend on that very person (1:29–34). He was there. Like the author of this exhortation (1 John), the Baptist sensed Jesus for who he was. He, the baptized one, is the Word of Life of today's reflection.

We are summoned by today's reading to sense Jesus, the person who stands behind the roles, the Jesus who got baptized, the Jesus who was superior to the Baptist, and the Jesus on whom the Spirit descended. The Christ is that Jesus. The Christ was the role given to the Son by the Father, but it was the Person behind the role who matters most.

QUESTIONS FOR REFLECTION
AND APPLICATION

1. As you begin this study, what do you hope to learn about Jesus? About the church? About yourself?

2. How does John appeal to the senses to explain his deep knowing of Jesus?

3. If John who wrote this exhortation is John the Apostle, what did he witness firsthand of Jesus?

4. What are the three ways we learn to know Jesus? Which has been most impactful to you?

5. With which of your senses do you most know Jesus?

FOR FURTHER READING

Fleming Rutledge, *The Bible and* The New York Times (Grand Rapids: Wm. B. Eerdmans, 1999).

THE SIX IFS OF LIFE

1 John 1:5–2:2

(reformatted)

⁵ This is the message we have heard from him and declare to you: God is light; in him there is no darkness at all.

⁶ If we claim to have fellowship with him and yet walk in the darkness, we lie and do not live out the truth.

⁷ But if we walk in the light, as he is in the light, we have fellowship with one another, and the blood of Jesus, his Son, purifies us from all sin.

⁸ If we claim to be without sin, we deceive ourselves and the truth is not in us.

⁹ If we confess our sins, he is faithful and just and will forgive us our sins and purify us from all unrighteousness.

10 If we claim we have not sinned, we make him out to be a liar and his word is not in us.

2:1 My dear children, I write this to you so that you will not sin.

But if anybody does sin, we have an advocate with the Father—Jesus Christ, the Righteous One. 2 He is the atoning sacrifice for our sins, and not only for ours but also for the sins of the whole world.

Christians sin. We could count the ways, but John will provide a threefold breakdown of our sins in 1 John 2:16:

The lust of the flesh
The lust of the eyes
The pride of life

In every generation of the church someone stands up to tell the church that he or she has discovered the path to never sinning again and that he or she is on that path. One of my family members, who is no longer with us, once informed me that she, a very strong Holiness Pentecostal, no longer sinned. Being a youthful theologian, I had some reasons for doubting her claims. So, when I overheard her gossiping on the phone and then pointed out what could be gossip by asking, "Isn't gossiping sin?" with nothing less than a kind smile on my face, she said to me, "Gossiping is a mistake, but not a sin." It was a fun, if not now rather revealing, point of view about sin itself. We can be confident John was not so generous in his understanding of sin. He knew that all believers sinned. The issue is not *if* believers sin (they do), but *what to do about sin in the Christian life.*

That lighthearted story about a family member masks a deeper issue I have witnessed time and time again. In the "let us count the ways" comment above, one could count more than a few pastors who have gotten caught in sin and done all they could to deny, deny, deny. In the past five years our family has heard dozens of stories about pastors having affairs or committing power abuse. Most of them don't fess up until they are cornered with undeniable truths. How, I have asked myself, can those who preach God's loving grace for sinners who admit their sins, when confronted with their own sins, refuse to admit that they have sinned? Pastors need to set the model for confession, not by hanging out their dirty laundry but by admitting weaknesses and sinfulness. John knows all Christians sin, *and* John knows Christians who don't want to confess their sins, and John knows that those who confess their sins will be graced with forgiveness. Those are the three themes of today's reflection of the *ifs* of this passage.

CHRISTIANS SIN

Those walking in the shadows when "God is light" (1:5; Psalm 76:4; 104:2) will have their sins exposed. John loves polarities, and one of his polarities is light and darkness (1 John 2:8–9), which are metaphors for God and sin. God is the light, God created the light (Genesis 1:3–5), God led

Israel with a light (Exodus 13:21), and David sang to God that God was his "lamp" and turned his "darkness into light" (2 Samuel 22:29). God's redemption gives "light to our eyes" (Ezra 9:8), and God's redemption involves tossing light into darkness (Job 12:22). The psalmist pleads for God to "let the light of your face shine on us" (Psalm 4:6; 13:3; 18:28), and God's law provides light (19:8; 119:105, 130), so the psalmist can announce, "Blessed are those who . . . walk in the light of your presence" (89:15). Isaiah urges his hearers to "walk in the light of the LORD" (Isaiah 2:5). When Jesus moved into Galilee the region saw and sensed a great light (Matthew 4:16), and when Jesus was transfigured, unveiling the fullness of who he was, he glowed (17:2). As such, in Jesus was not only "life," but the life he was and brought was "the light of all mankind" (John 1:4, 9).

John's Gospel sets the imagery for John's exhortation, and this is the warning of Jesus echoed in 1 John: "This is the verdict: Light has come into the world, but people loved darkness instead of light because their deeds were evil. Everyone who does evil hates the light, and will not come into the light for fear that their deeds will be exposed. But whoever lives by the truth comes into the light, so that it may be seen plainly that what they have done has been done in the sight of God" (John 3:19–21; cf. 12:35–36). The light that has come into the world is Jesus (8:12; 9:5; 12:46). No wonder when Paul met Jesus on the road to Damascus, Jesus was pure light (Acts 9:3). That God in Christ *is* the true Light urges us to embrace that God determines what is light. As Karen Jobes writes, "That it is God himself who defines spiritual light, and darkness is perhaps the foremost principle that seekers and converts to Christianity need to embrace" (Jobes, *1–3 John*, 73). Notice her words: embracing the darkness reveals that we embrace the Light itself.

Seeing the light is a sensate experience. So is noticing the darkness. Those who have constant access to all the light they need—as most of us do—can become so familiar with the sensate experience that they fail to experience it. But once we are deprived of light long enough for it to become uncomfortable and even hazardous, we become aware of the sensory experience of darkness. That experience makes us aware of the sensory experience of light again. If we dwell in darkness, we will grow numb to it. We may also avoid the light, like Gollum. We may hide in the dark corners to escape the light. We have five senses: seeing, hearing, smelling, touching, and tasting. A sixth sense is one the Bible exposes us to all the time: God. Christians sense God. David de Silva once asked in a sermon this question: "Do you exercise this God-sense regularly?" He then expressed a wish: "I wish that I could say that my sense of God was always open, that I was as constantly aware of God's presence as I'm aware of the sound if there's music playing or people talking or that I was as constantly aware of God's prompting as I'm aware of the first whiff of cookies baking" (de Silva, *In and Out of Season*, 68).

Light exposes what is hidden in darkness. There are two responses to the light's exposure: embrace it or reject it. John spells out both. Those who are Christians that sin are walking in darkness while claiming to be in the light. If we do that, John exhorts his readers, we "falsify and don't do the Truth" (1 John 1:6; *Second Testament*). Judith Lieu observes the depth of John's language when she writes, "Lying belongs to darkness as truth belongs to light" (Lieu, *1–3 John*, 54). John draws his readers into conditions, and the sensitive reader will be asking, *Which one applies to me?* He draws us in by using six *ifs* in our passage (I put them in italics in the translation). Here is a list of three *ifs* that pertain to living in sin:

> *If* we claim to have fellowship with him and yet walk in
> the darkness, we lie and do not live out the truth.
> *If* we claim to be without sin, we deceive ourselves and
> the truth is not in us.
> *If* we claim we have not sinned, we make him out to be
> a liar and his word is not in us.

Three claims are made here: that sin doesn't matter one hoot in our relationship with God and others; that a person can be entirely sinless; and that a person has never sinned. Each of these claims reveals a person living an illusory relationship with God. Something else surfaces: each of these claims denies the fundamental reality of the Christian faith, which is that God has come to us in Christ to redeem us from sin's darkness. Denial of sin makes a person incapable of participating in the faith. Eugene Peterson once preached that two sorts of people have the most trouble admitting their sins: the independent and the selfish. "The successfully independent person has no good concept of sin because, as far as he can tell, he has no relationships that are important to him, so flaws and such relationships don't affect him much. And the successfully selfish person has no good concept of sin because she is so skilled at getting the people around her to fulfill her personal desires that she is not bothered by the possibility that the relationships are flawed" (Peterson, *Lights a Lovely Mile*, 167–168).

Christians sin; Christian leaders sin. If Christians deny they have ever sinned, have not sinned, or do not sin, (1) they are walking in darkness, (2) they are falsifying the truth, (3) they are not living out the truth, (4) they are self-deceived, (5) they make God out to be a liar, and (6) the word of God's truth is not in them. So, it's very serious business for the Christian not to admit sin. Again, Jobes writes, "My role as a creature of God is to bend my will to his, to walk in the light as he has defined it, and to live with the moral consequences of my decisions" (Jobes, *1–3 John*, 73). So, Christians sin. John wants us to start there.

CHRISTIANS CONFESS

Sinning Christians are to confess their sins. The problem for some is figuring out what actually constitutes sinning. Perhaps Nancy Mairs, a wonderful essayist, can help. She reflected on what sin is like this: "I have come to apprehend sin as the state into which I'm thrown whenever I choose, consciously or not, to act in a manner that frays or severs the bonds of love between me and my fellow creatures, between me and the God present to me through those creatures"

(Mairs, *Ordinary Time*, 126). We can all fit easily into the definition.

Confession and relationship with God are intertwined. Confession begins with self-examination and admission, and admission begins with reception of the light's exposure of the darkness. At times the light shines on a person and the person deflects the light—making excuses, minimizing the sin. At times the person is innocent and shines light back that is rejected. At times the person embraces the light and admits the darkness. Constantine Campbell offers simple words for us: "There is nothing to be gained . . . by pretending [not to confess our sins] since God already knows the truth. But there is much to be gained by honest and repentant confession" (Campbell, *1–3 John*, 41). Confession of sin reflects genuineness of relationship with the light. Without it we end up in darkness. Or, as Bonhoeffer famously put it, "Cheap grace is preaching forgiveness without repentance; it is baptism without the discipline of community; it is the Lord's Supper without confession of sin; it is absolution without personal confession" (Bonhoeffer, *Discipleship*, 44). Christians are confessors of sin.

Christians throughout the world have a good habit when on Sundays they gather together and confess their sins. Here is one of the best confessions the church has ever framed into words:

Most merciful God,
we confess that we have sinned against you
in thought, word, and deed,
by what we have done,
and by what we have left undone.
We have not loved you with our whole heart;
we have not loved our neighbors as ourselves.
We are truly sorry and we humbly repent.
For the sake of your Son Jesus Christ,
have mercy on us and forgive us;
that we may delight in your will,
and walk in your ways,
to the glory of your Name. Amen.
  (From "A Penitential Order: Rite Two" in the Book of
  Common Prayer; *see For Further Reading for link)*

My experience has shown that those who are nurtured into a faith that routinely confesses its sins together in this prayer of confession can more easily admit their sins when they are discovered. The words John uses for admitting sins include "walk in the light" (1:7) and "confess our sins" (1:9).

To walk in the light means to be exposed by the God who is Light, by the Jesus who is the Light, both to *who* God is and *who* we truly are. That is, that we are humans made in God's image who deface the image by sin. Admitting that, in specifics and in generalities, is genuine confession. So, we are to confess our impatience and our mistreatments, our overruling passions and our lusts, our greed and our covetousness, our misuses of power and our abuse of others. The light of God has shone upon the evangelical church in the last decade, and some speak of a divine reckoning. Into one corner of this divine reckoning my daughter, Laura Barringer, and I have spoken with our books *A Church Called Tov* and *Pivot*. What was hidden in darkness—power and sexual abuse—has been exposed to the light. Language, like spiritual abuse, now exposes what church leaders have gotten away with for decades and centuries. We have received blowback from leaders who don't like the terms. One pastor announced that he didn't know any pastors who couldn't be accused of spiritual abuse. While I would like to contend that he's mistaken on this count, what grieved me was that the pastor trumpeted his words as if "spiritual abuse" is a lighthearted and foolish set of terms. So, here is the definition Laura and I have written about when it comes to spiritual abuse:

> Spiritual abuse is a form of emotional and psychological abuse, characterized by a systematic pattern of coercive and controlling behavior in a religious context. Spiritual abuse can have a deeply damaging impact on those who experience it. This abuse may include:
>
> - manipulation and exploitation
> - enforced accountability
> - censorship of decision-making
> - requirements for secrecy and silence
> - coercion to conform [inability to ask questions]
> - control through the use of sacred texts or teaching

- requirement of obedience to the abuser
- the suggestion that the abuser has a "divine" position
- isolation as a means of punishment
- superiority and elitism[*]

When confronted with the truth of spiritual abuse, the one walking in the light will never make light of it. Instead, the person will admit the truth, confess sins, and enter into a process of redemptive healing, reconciliation, and restoration.

Christians sin. Christians walking in the light confess their sins. The goodness of God leads to redemptive forgiveness.

CHRISTIANS ARE FORGIVEN

The ifs of confession lead to the following goodnesses:

But *if* we walk in the light, as he is in the light, we have fellowship with one another, and the blood of Jesus, his Son, purifies us from all sin.

If we confess our sins, he is faithful and just and will forgive us our sins and purify us from all unrighteousness.

But *if* anybody does sin, we have an advocate with the Father—Jesus Christ, the Righteous One. He is the atoning sacrifice for our sins, and not only for ours but also for the sins of the whole world.

---

[*] *Lisa Oakley and Justin Humphreys,* Escaping Spiritual Abuse: Creating Healthy Christian Cultures *(London: SPCK, 2019), 31. This definition originally published at Lisa Oakley, "Understanding Spiritual Abuse," Church Times 16 February, www.churchtimes .co.uk/articles/2018/16-february/comment/opinion/understanding-spiritual-abuse.*

Because Jesus is the "atoning sacrifice" (2:2), or the "means of mercy for our sins" (*Second Testament*), Jesus provides forgiveness for all sins. His life for our life, his death instead of our death. The term has been translated with propitiation, which means averting God's wrath against sinners; as expiation, which refers to wiping the slate clean of sin and guilt; and as a mercy seat, which refers to the place or person where God reveals and enacts his mercy for humans. This text does not mention or imply God's wrath. Instead, the term about sacrifice pertains to removing sin and purifying sinners of pollution.

The blood of Jesus, like blood in the temple (Leviticus 16:15–19), purifies us, making it possible for God to dwell with us and us with God. As humans responsible for our sins, we are summoned to confess sins in order to know Jesus' redemptive graces. Jesus as such is the "advocate," a term in John's Gospel for the Holy Spirit (John 14:16), but in 1 John it is used for Jesus. Since John says Jesus will send another advocate, Jesus is the original advocate. The image of advocate here is not that Jesus is pleading on our behalf, which he has already accomplished by his death and resurrection. As the just, or righteous, Advocate, Jesus both illuminates us because he is the Light and provides forgiveness for the illuminated. In John 14–16, the Spirit's advocacy is more of one who is the "Illuminator" (*Second Testament*), but in 1 John the Son as advocate is one who mercifully wipes away sin.

We not only then have an Advocate who covers us with mercy, but our admission and confession of sins leads to forgiveness and purification (1:7, 9). The magnificence of this forgiveness escorts us into the fellowship of the Father and Son and Spirit (1:3), which means it also escorts us into renewed fellowship with one another, that is with the one-anothers who are in fellowship with God (1:7). Horizontal fellowship and divine fellowship are integrated into one another.

This is the "message" John heard from "him," that is, from Jesus (1:5), the Jesus John knew through his senses (cf. Matthew 6:14–15; 18:1–35). The expansiveness of that sensate knowing explains how he knows that Jesus is the means of mercy not only for these believers but for the "sins of the whole world" (1 John 2:2).

QUESTIONS FOR REFLECTION AND APPLICATION

1. What are the three false claims a Christian can make about sin?

2. Consider Nancy Mairs' definition of sin as acting "in a manner that frays or severs the bonds of love." Do you agree or disagree, and why?

3. What does John promise is possible for believers in Jesus when they confess their sins?

4. Since grace is available for those who confess their sins, why do you think so many Christians still struggle to confess?

5. Are there any sins that you tend to think of as "mistakes" instead of "sins"?

FOR FURTHER READING

Dietrich Bonhoeffer, *Discipleship*, Dietrich
Bonhoeffer Works 4 (Minneapolis: Fortress,
2001).

David de Silva, *In and Out of Season: Sermons for
the Christian Year* (Bellingham, Washington:
Lexham, 2019).

Nancy Mairs, *Ordinary Time: Cycles in Marriage,
Faith, and Renewal* (Boston: Beacon, 1993).

The Penitential Order of *The Book of Common
Prayer*: https://en.wikisource.org/wiki/Book_
of_Common_Prayer_(ECUSA)/The_Holy_
Eucharist/A_Penitential_Order:_Rite_Two.

Eugene Peterson, *Lights a Lovely Mile: Collected
Sermons of the Church Year* (Colorado Springs:
WaterBrook, 2023).

THE LOVE OF LIFE

1 John 2:3–11

[3] *We know that we have come to know him if we keep his commands.* [4] *Whoever says, "I know him," but does not do what he commands is a liar, and the truth is not in that person.* [5] *But if anyone obeys his word, love for God is truly made complete in them. This is how we know we are in him:* [6] *Whoever claims to live in him must live as Jesus did.*

[7] *Dear friends, I am not writing you a new command but an old one, which you have had since the beginning. This old command is the message you have heard.* [8] *Yet I am writing you a new command; its truth is seen in him and in you, because the darkness is passing and the true light is already shining.*

[9] *Anyone who claims to be in the light but hates a brother or sister is still in the darkness.* [10] *Anyone who loves their brother and sister lives in the light, and there is nothing in them to make them stumble.* [11] *But anyone who hates a brother or sister is in the darkness and walks around in the darkness. They do not know where they are going, because the darkness has blinded them.*

Tie these three strands into our Celtic-like knot: knowing, loving, doing. Knowing God means loving God, and knowing and loving God means doing what God commands. Obeying God is loving God, and through loving we know God. John is concerned about identifying the true believer. John's exhortation knows the indicators of genuine faith.

The rock band Foreigner expresses the ache of wanting to know what love is in these words:

> I wanna know what love is
> I want you to show me
> I wanna feel what love is
> I know you can show me

Whitney Houston echoed Foreigner's quest with "How Will I Know," but her exploration leads to no certain answer. (I apologize if one of these songs bounces around in your head the rest of the day.) It is not foolish or faddish to connect interpersonal romantic, emotional love with our love for God. Nor should we pretend God's love for us is unlike romantic love. It was family love, even emotional, erotic love, that gave rise to language about our relationship with God. Moses informs us that "the LORD set his affection" on Israel (and us, Deuteronomy 10:15), and the very term used (*hashaq*) is a term used for the affective, erotic love between a woman and a man, as in Genesis 34:8: "My son Shechem *has his heart set on* your daughter" (emphasis added), Hamor said. In an excellent study of God's love, a Jewish expert on the Hebrew

Bible believes this language means that God *fell in love* with Israel (Levenson, *Love of God*). When our intimate love for one another does what is right, our love echoes the love God has for us. There is a reason why the love celebrated in the Song of Solomon comprehends both marital love and divine-human love.

While we may project our terms for our experience of love onto God, God's love is first, which means that our love is but an echo of God's love for us, not the other way around. The prophet Hosea (chapters 1–3) reveals a God who is madly in love with Israel, but also a God who knows what it means to be a spurned lover when love is understood as allegiance and faithfulness. All of these factor into John's use of love in our reading. It is a pity that at times in the church some have said love in the Christian sense is not an emotion, or that love's feelings and love's rational thinking are opposites. Such persons claim, mistakenly, that love is an action. Not only does this view fail to understand how love is used in the Bible (see above), but it fails to understand how vital emotions are to how we think, feel, and act. Emotion-less love is not love. It is cold calculation.

Love, as we have defined in the *New Testament Everyday Bible Study Series*, is a rugged, affective commitment to be with a person (presence) and to be for a person (advocacy) in order for both lover and beloved to grow together in virtue (direction), or Christlikeness or Christoformity. The importance of love in 1 John cannot be overstated. While in 2:1 he addresses his audience with "my children," in 2:7 the same audience is "loved ones" (*Second Testament*). God is love, Jesus reveals God's love, we are to love God, and we are to love one another—hence, as the one pastoring this community in this communiqué, John

31

addresses them as "loved ones" because he loves them as God has loved him. Love (*agapē, agapaō*) is used in the Gospel of John and 1 John just shy of one hundred times, which is about one-half of the uses in the entire New Testament.

LOVE LIVES LIKE JESUS

John does not define the "him" and "his" of verse three: "We know that we have come to know *him* if we keep *his* commands." However, not only were verses one and two about Jesus, but to know God is to know Jesus and to know Jesus is to know God. So, it is reasonable to think "him" and "his" are Jesus, but it is just as reasonable to think they refer to God. And, "knowing God is the most essential kind of human knowledge" (Jobes, *1–3 John*, 89). In today's reading (1 John 2:3, 5), to know Jesus is to keep or observe his teachings. The same Greek word stands behind the NIV's translations: keep, obey (2:3, 5). The essence of Jesus' teachings, according to Jesus himself, is to love God and to love others as we love ourselves (Matthew 22:34–40). John adds to "trust in the name" of Jesus (1 John 3:23, *Second Testament*). Thus, obeying the "word" of Jesus results in a "love for God [that] is truly made complete" (1 John 2:5). "Love," Constantine Campbell writes, "shapes our will." That is, "If we truly love God we will live his way" (Campbell, *1–3 John*, 65). John likes to tumble forward with new ideas, which is why he then says knowing, loving, and obeying means living "as Jesus did" (2:6), or as in *The Second Testament*, "to walk around" as Jesus "walked around." The image is physical; John exhorts us to have a concrete life that looks like Jesus walking around in Galilee.

You can start from this last line and read the whole of 2:3–6 from the angle of living like Jesus. To know Jesus, to love Jesus, and to obey Jesus is to live life like Jesus. To live like Jesus is to live a life of love. The ultimate quest to understand love that singers pursue, when properly pursued, leads to the ultimate of loves: God is love, God loves, we learn love from God in Christ, and we participate in God's love when we learn to love God and love others as we love ourselves. So, Foreigner's wish for the lover to "show me" what love is echoes that God did show us divine love: He sent his Son, and in Jesus we know God's love. To love God is to love Jesus. John would say we cannot love God without loving Jesus. "Union with one is union with both" (Bennett, *1–3 John*, 23).

"Grandma Theology"

In the late 1970s, Black seminarians at Perkins School of Theology at Southern Methodist University in Dallas began to describe their theology as "Grandma Theology." Their goal was to express their theology in terms that any African American grandmother with a third-grade education could understand and hopefully affirm with a strong "Amen!" John attempts to do the same thing for his readers. The book is relatively free of technical terms and repeats traditional expressions important to the community. In this way, John wants his readers to say "Amen!" to his message to them.

Thomas B. Slater, "1–3 John," 533.

Love Looks Like Jesus

John is unafraid of repetition, but his repetitions are not rigid. They are variations and explorations of a theme, like an expert examining a single diamond from all sides, with light bouncing around to reveal the mystery and glory of the gem. John holds love in his hand and looks at it from two sides in verses seven through eight. Love of God and others can perhaps be called "old" because we find it from the "beginning" with Moses (Deuteronomy 6:4–8). Or it can be called "old" because Jesus gave it to the disciples while he was ministering to them on earth (cf. 1 John 3:11). Or it is "old" because it was with them from the day of their conversion (2:7). But love can simultaneously be called "new" because Jesus gave Moses a new life with what I have called the "Jesus Creed" (Mark 12:28–34; cf. John 13:34–35). Khaled Anatolios, in one of his sermons, puts it like this: "Yet, when we turn again to our Lord Jesus Christ, in whom Love itself became flesh, he makes it again a new commandment for us by making us capable of the ever-new life of loving God and loving each other through him and in the power of his Spirit" (Anatolios, *Feasts for the Kingdom*, 11).

The "truth" of the new command to love "is seen in him [Jesus]" (1 John 2:8). In Jesus the "true light is already shining." In Jesus we see love and light, and that means true love looks like Jesus, and Jesus makes the old love new. Everything is tied together as in a Celtic knot.

Marking John's Themes

A suggestion for you: find a different way to mark the
following themes in 1 John:

Love, light, life, sin, world, hatred, believing/faith,
truth, knowing

Some might add to these God, Father, Son/Jesus/Jesus
Christ, Spirit.

Read through the whole of 1 John in one sitting and
mark each of these terms as it appears. You may need
to do this more than once to get them all. When you
are done you will have a (very) marked-up copy of 1
John in which you'll be able to see how John's the-
matic terms shape the whole of 1 John. A marked-up
copy of 1 John reveals what I mean by a Celtic knot:
the themes are inseparable.

Try writing four sentences in which two of the
following nouns occur in each sentence: love, life,
know, truth, command, light. Try to use the verbs:
love, live, know, or command.

LOVE WALKS IN THE LIGHT

Anchoring the new command in Jesus as the true light who is
"already shining" sets John off into love as a life of walking in
the light. Mentioning light leads him to think of its opposite,

darkness. John can be ambiguous at times, but he can also scratch deep lines in the sand because he knows there are only two paths: one is the path of light and the other is the path of darkness. The darkness path is a life of hating; the light path is a life of love. Those who find themselves hating "a brother or sister" (2:9, 11) are in the darkness. The actual term is "brother" (*adelphos*), but it is an inclusive brother, which is why I translate it as "sibling" in *The Second Testament*, though I find the NIV's decision to use brother and sister perfectly reasonable. John sees believers as a family, and what he is most concerned about is family fractures resulting from leaving the light of love and entering the darkness of hate. As Thomas Bennett warns us, "A believer who allows hatred and schism to take root has abandoned the very core of the Son's command and is as blind . . . as one who has never known the light revealed in the Son at all" (Bennett, *1–3 John*, 30).

Light in 1 John

1 John 1:5 *This is the message we have heard from him and declare to you: God is light; in him there is no darkness at all.*

1 John 1:7 *But if we walk in the light, as he is in the light, we have fellowship with one another, and the blood of Jesus, his Son, purifies us from all sin.*

> **1 John 2:8** *Yet I am writing you a new command; its truth is seen in him and in you, because the darkness is passing and the true light is already shining.*
>
> **1 John 2:9–10** *Anyone who claims to be in the light but hates a brother or sister is still in the darkness. Anyone who loves their brother and sister lives in the light, and there is nothing in them to make them stumble.*

To hate is to despise, to disregard, to foster anti-feelings against someone, to want them to experience pain and evil and alienation. Any forms of hatred toward one's siblings in Christ indicate that the hater is walking outside of Christ in the darkness. To live in the light is to love the siblings—all siblings. That means Roman Catholic and Eastern Orthodox and Pentecostals and Baptists and Presbyterians and non- or un-denominational sorts and house church folks. "Perhaps we struggle to love believers of different races and ethnicities" (M. Echevarría, "1–3 John," 712). Perhaps slides into "Surely" for too many. Loving our siblings in Christ is one of the Christian's most demanding challenges. We may disagree with our siblings, but underneath and over all our disagreements love for one another must shape our lives. Which means sharing communion, worshiping with one another, and praying with and for one another.

A pervasive sin among Christians is tribalism, which shows up in such small matters as refusing to "Like" a person's Facebook or Instagram or X or Threads update but also in degrading language about the other. Sometimes that language is passive-aggressive—saying something without saying it explicitly when others know exactly what is intended. And sometimes the behaviors are overt—like intentionally and publicly denouncing someone. Kathleen Norris dipped her exquisite pen into this theme when she wrote, "There will always be some in this world who want their holy wars, who will discriminate, vilify, and even kill in the name of God. They have narrowed down the concept of neighbor to include only those like themselves, in terms of creed, caste, race, sex, or sexual orientation. But there is also much evidence that there are many who know that a neighbor might be anyone at all and are willing to act on that assumption" (Norris, *Amazing Grace*, 354–355).

Here's what it means to walk in the light: *If that person has a relationship to Christ, that person deserves my love, my prayers, my compassion, and my attempts to get along.* To refuse any of these is to walk in darkness; it is to choose to walk away from the Light, who is Jesus. *If Jesus embraces them, so should I.* Jesus has long arms, longer than any of us have. Having said this, I must also add some words of concern: some people are not safe to be around—and Jesus may love them, but we are wise to hold off until some conditions are met. To love others does not mean intentionally or even unintentionally putting ourselves in situations with Christian siblings where we can be abused or degraded by them. God's grace over time can heal relationships, but there are times for healing that include separation and distance.

QUESTIONS FOR REFLECTION
AND APPLICATION

1. What do you think of the idea that God is "in love" with God's people?

2. If love in the Bible is actually an emotion and not just a rational action, how does this impact your reading of passages about love?

3. What is the mark of knowing Jesus according to John in today's reading?

4. How do you know that you love Jesus?

5. Do you have a relationship with a Christian sibling in which love needs to look like forgiveness and possibly reconciliation? Do you have a relationship in which love needs to look like wise and safe distance?

FOR FURTHER READING

Khaled Anatolios, *Feasts for the Kingdom* (Grand Rapids: Wm. B. Eerdmans, 2023).

Foreigner: Album: *Street Thunder* (B side), 1984. Atlantic. Author: Mick Jones, Lou Gramm. Songwriters: Michael Jones. "I Want to Know What Love Is" lyrics © Somerset Songs Publishing Inc., Somerset Songs Publishing.

Whitney Houston: Album: *Whitney Houston* (B side), 1985. Arista. Author: George Merrill, et al.

Jon Levenson, *The Love of God: Divine Gift, Human Gratitude, and Mutual Faithfulness in Judaism* (Princeton: Princeton University Press, 2016).

For a deep dive into the Bible's senses of love, I highly recommend Patrick Mitchel, *The Message of Love*, The Bible Speaks Today (London: IVP, 2019).

Kathleen Norris, *Amazing Grace: A Vocabulary of Faith* (New York: Riverhead, 19d F98).

RESISTING WORLDLINESS IN THIS LIFE

1 John 2:12–17

[12] I am writing to you, dear children [teknía],
because your sins have been forgiven on account of his
name.
[13] I am writing to you, fathers,
because you know him who is from the beginning.
I am writing to you, young men,
because you have overcome the evil one.
[14] I write to you, dear children [paidia],
because you know the Father.
I write to you, fathers,
because you know him who is from the beginning.
I write to you, young men,
because you are strong,
and the word of God lives in you,
and you have overcome the evil one.

> *15 Do not love the world or anything in the world. If any-*
> *one loves the world, love for the Father is not in them.*
> *16 For everything in the world—the lust of the flesh, the*
> *lust of the eyes, and the pride of life—comes not from the*
> *Father but from the world. 17 The world and its desires*
> *pass away, but whoever does the will of God lives forever.*

Note: the underlined terms are past tense. Thus, "wrote"
more accurately reveals John's own use of terms.

God's will for you and for me is simple: we are to love
God, we are to love ourselves, and we are to love
others. We are to live in an interactive union with one
another. Sometimes loving others leads to necessary, if also
tragic, fractures (2:19). But loving one another is the life God
designed for us, and living a life of love leads us into the
light. Love turns the threads of the Celtic knot into a knot-
less unity. The gospel challenges us to exit the world with its
darkness and to enter into the family of God where we find
the power to overcome the world each day. The world and
its system resists every human's attempt to love God, to love
ourselves, and to love others.

The world is invisible to us because it is the air we breathe.
Its voice silently careens from one end of the world's echo chamber to the other. It is the only voice that penetrates us without
our hearing it. The longer we live in the world the more difficult it is to hear any other voice. Into this world the Logos of
God, Jesus Christ, breaks in with an alternative voice, a new
sound, and fresh words of redemption. But the first challenge
is to recognize the world. It is nearly indetectable, complex,

complicated, networked, stifling, silencing, and oppressing. Like racism, sexism, materialism, capitalism. Like the color of water to fish, the color of air to birds, the color of dirt to worms. Worldliness is our native language. It has taught us who we are, who we can become, where we are headed, and who others are. The world is a poison that robs us of true life and the goodnesses of God's love. The world's aim is death and destruction and degradation. The world snips the threads in the Celtic knot John forms. How can we discern the world? John helps immensely. More than any other writer in the Bible.

We need to ponder the all-pervasive influence of the world on us. Our personal spending has been shaped either by a conscious effort to follow Jesus or by efforts to resist the world's systems. Our personal identity has been formed either by the world's status and pride systems or who we are in God. What we devote our time to breathes either the air of the world or the air of knowing God. We might ask ourselves, How much time with God, God's people, and the Bible do we need to become capable discerners of the world's impact on us? Because our passage reveals that the world is the challenge, and even though it comes at the end of today's reading, we begin with the world.

THE WORLD

John's world and ours join hands in that both prevent believers from living a life in this world that differs from the world. The term "world" occurs seventeen times in 1 John.* Many of

---

* *1 John 2:2, 15, 16, 17; 3:1, 13, 17; 4:1, 3, 4, 5, 9, 14, 17; 5:4, 5, 19. Sometimes the term appears more than once in a verse.*

us lack a theology of the "world" today, and a serious concern with the marks of worldliness may cause raised eyebrows with others. Here is a sketch of ten points about the world and worldliness in 1 John:

1. The world is God's creation that has come under the grip of the evil one (5:19; 4:1, 9, 17);
2. the world has become a self-perpetuating system of sinfulness that has us in its grip (2:16; 3:17; 4:5; 5:19);
3. the world is disordered desire that emerges from our fallen nature and becomes active by our sight (2:16);
4. the world prompts us to want more and more of what we can get out of life (2:16; 3:17);
5. the world is anti-God (2:15, 16; 3:1);
6. the world is anti-Christ (4:3);
7. the world is anti-believers (3:1, 13);
8. the world is loved by God (4:9), and the world has been atoned for through Jesus the Savior (2:2; 4:14);
9. the world has been defeated for us (4:4, 5; 5:4);
10. the world is fading away (2:17).

The world, even though created by God, has become a Satan-captured, self-perpetuating system of opposition to the truth of God (light, life, love) in Christ and is thus an echo chamber of self-congratulations. We live in a world that provides for us a fleshly nature and, as such, the world is against what God designed us for. But this world's system has been overcome by Jesus, who died on the cross to conquer sin and defeat the evil one. The primary weapons of the evil one's worldly system are desires contrary to God's will and the drive for status shaped by resources and possessions. That great Methodist scholar C. K. Barrett, in a sermon he preached fourteen times, said what we need to hear: "For most of us, the danger is not [in the total collapse of our faith and morals, like celebrity Christians] . . . it lies rather in the gradual accommodating of ourselves to standards which are not much, but just a little lower than Christian" (C. K. Barrett, *Luminescence* 2.307). The "standards" about which he speaks are the world's standards.

Let us dip down a bit into some of these marks of worldliness. John shapes his teachings about the world by a rhetoric of either-or: either God or the world. He knows nuances but he also knows that when one wants to exhort and persuade, the either-or approach effectively speaks into the heart. First, he wants those who walk in the light to know that darkness is real and that the darkness of this world derives from the evil one (5:19 with 4:1, 9, 17), thus framing life in this world as a cosmic war zone. Second, for John the world is an agent, and it could be spelled with an uppercase *W*, as in World. The world is a self-perpetuating system of sin. It may take time, or it may be noticed immediately, but once you enter its war zone you sense it in your heart, in your soul, in your mind, in your lack of freedom. We can become so worldly that we don't recognize the world's grip on us.

Third, John provides three clear signs of worldliness in 2:16. They are (1) the desire that derives from the flesh, that is, physical desires; (2) the desire that is sparked by the eyes, that is, a desire for what we see and a desire to live up to what others see (reputation, honor, glory, status); and (3) a pride in getting "more and more out of life" (*Second Testament*). A very Ephesian thing to do, by the way (Glahn, *Ephesus*, 15–21). While we are accustomed to connect "desire" (or "lust" in the NIV) with "flesh" and think of flaunting sensualities, sexual immorality, adultery, pornography, and addictions, John expands desire from what comes from the "flesh" to what is sparked by the "eyes." Eye-desire prompts us to want what others can see, what others think of us, what others think is greatness or glorious and famous and celebrity. For a first-century Christian in Ephesus or Philippi the monuments and statues of the famous sent images through the eyes into the mind and heart of what made a person acceptable, worthy, and honorable. In our day it is numbers of likes and views on social media, that once-in-a-lifetime presence on a TV program, the size of our house, the location of one's vacations, the frequency of invitations to tony parties, and for authors (like me) it is who said what about a book I wrote.

That third item calls for comment, too. A more wooden translation (from *Second Testament*) of each looks like this: "wanting more and more out of life" (2:16) and "whoever has Kosmos's life" (3:17). The NIV clarifies by getting more specific than the Greek text with "the pride of life" (2:16) and "if anyone has material possessions" (3:17). The word that requires nuance is *bios*, often translated as "life", but it has the sense of one's course in life, one's choice of how to live. We get our word *biography* from the Greek term. Number three then adds "pride" or boasting or desiring more and more. The idea is *pretense*, a pride in one's presentation of oneself. Now we're talking social media at its heart, for where else does one curate one's image more directly and consciously? Those who have learned to play the self-branding game successfully, that is, in the eyes of the world, may well be driven to exhibit this "pride of life."

Our final comment about world is how opposed it is to God in Christ. This is where the term "antichrist" comes from. By the way, "antichrist" is not found in the book of Revelation. We find the term five times in the New Testament, four of them in 1 John (2:18 [twice], 22; 4:3) and one in 2 John 7. Antichrist fits any and every person who denies the truth that Jesus is the Messiah and God is the Father. Antichrists reveal the darknesses of the days.

IN THE WORLD

We all live in the world. The challenge is to live in the world but not be worldly. The challenge is to love God, and that means doing the "will of God" (2:17). John knows that his exhortations need to be addressed to three groups: children (for whom he uses two terms (*teknía* in 2:12 and *paidía* in 2:14), fathers (2:13, 14), and either young ones or young men (2:13, 14). A very important word in our passage is "because." It is *because of* specific acts of God's redemption that the children and fathers and young ones/men need to hear the challenges of worldliness. What they need to hear is that they have participated in the exodus from the world. But let's pause for this: in "children" John speaks to the entire audience, not to small children. This term (*teknía*) occurs for the whole audience clearly in 2:28; 3:7, 18; 4:4, and 5:21. Its kissing cousin, *paidia*, is used the same way in 2:18. So, "children" is John's term for his congregation (as it were). We will see the same in 2 John (1, 13) and 3 John (4). He speaks to fathers either as physical fathers who need pastoral exhortation or as the mature adult believers in the audience. I am unsure whether "young men" or "young ones" forms the better translation. The term *neaniskoi* is masculine, so young *men* is a natural translation. The term occurs eleven times in the New Testament, and every other time it does refer to a young man/men (e.g., Matthew 19:20; Luke 7:14; Acts 2:17). We could broaden it for the sake of our audiences to be "young ones," but John's term probably refers to the young men. Evidently the fathers and young men needed some special attention, even though everybody gets addressed with "children." But we should consider that what is said concerning these three groups is said to the whole church elsewhere in this letter. This suggests what is said in 2:12–14 applies to everyone. For example, notice that all who believe are born of God and that all born of God have overcome the world (5:1, 4). Thomas Bennett thinks the direct addresses in 1 John (children, fathers, loved ones) "always refer to the entire family of God"! (Bennett, *1–3 John*, 38).

Terms for John's Addressees

Dear friends (*agapētoi*): 2:7; 3:2, 21; 4:1, 7, 11

Dear children (*teknía, paidia*, teknon*): 2:1, 12, 14*, 18*,
    28; 3:*1, 2,* 7, *10,* 18; 4:4; 5:*2,* 21

Fathers, young ones/men: 2:13, 14

Siblings/brothers/brothers and sisters: 2:9, 10, 11; 3:10,
    12, 13, 14, 15, 16, 17; 4:20, 21; 5:16

Now on to *because*. They can all resist worldliness *because* God has forgiven their sins (2:12) and *because* they all now know God the Father (2:14). The fathers can resist the world *because* they "know him who is from the beginning," which refers either to God the Creator or to the Jesus they have known from their conversion (2:13, 14). The young ones/men can challenge the world *because* they have "overcome the evil one" in the work of Christ (2:13). In addition to their victory in Christ, the young ones/men can fight off worldliness *because* they are "strong" and *because* "God's Logos remains in" them (2:14, *Second Testament*).

Let this be our reminder to close down today's reading: we are empowered to resist worldliness today, not because of who we are, not because of our giftedness or education, *but **only** because God's gracious love has come our way in Christ, redeemed us, and indwells us to empower us to victory over the world.* "We are not the artists of our own beauty," so says Constantine Campbell (*1–3 John*, 83). In Christ we are in the process of being transformed into Christoformity, or Christlikeness. Our reminder then sums up John's poignant words: "Do not love the world or anything in the world" (2:15).

QUESTIONS FOR REFLECTION AND APPLICATION

1. How would you summarize what John means by "the world"?

2. What are three signs of worldliness John points out?

3. What is an "antichrist" in John's writing?

4. Why do you think John refers to his congregation as "dear children"?

5. What do you find most challenging about resisting the world?

FOR FURTHER READING

C. K. Barrett, *Luminescence: The Sermons of C. K. and Fred Barrett*, volume 2, ed. Bem Witherington III (Eugene, Oregon: Cascade, 2017).

DEFECTIONS
FROM THE LIFE

1 John 2:18–27

[18] *Dear children, this is the last hour; and as you have heard that the antichrist is coming, even now many antichrists have come. This is how we know it is the last hour.* [19] *They went out from us, but they did not really belong to us. For if they had belonged to us, they would have remained with us; but their going showed that none of them belonged to us.*

[20] *But you have an anointing from the Holy One, and all of you know the truth.* [21] *I do not write to you because you do not know the truth, but because you do know it and because no lie comes from the truth.* [22] *Who is the liar? It is whoever denies that Jesus is the Christ. Such a person is the antichrist—denying the Father and the Son.* [23] *No one who denies the Son has the Father; whoever acknowledges the Son has the Father also.*

[24] *As for you, see that what you have heard from the beginning remains in you. If it does, you also will*

> remain in the Son and in the Father. [25] And this is what he promised us—eternal life.
>
> [26] I am writing these things to you about those who are trying to lead you astray. [27] As for you, the anointing you received from him remains in you, and you do not need anyone to teach you. But as his anointing teaches you about all things and as that anointing is real, not counterfeit—just as it has taught you, remain in him.

There are differences among us. Some differences steer us into defections. Defections happen. Defections reveal. Some defectors abandon the truth of the gospel, and it is in their leaving that the truth about their allegiance to Jesus Christ is revealed. Today's reading begins with this second kind of defection. John can't quite let the dangers of defection go, but in today's reading he does move gently forward with nothing less than a supernatural gift that prevents the truly allegiant from defecting. Not all defections reveal. And especially not all defections reveal "antichrist." Some do. John is all about those that do. Today's text moves from the antichrists to the anointing, which itself is revealing, and what it reveals is who is living the true life. The anointing is rooted in what they *know* because they are indwelt by God. Once again, John's terms form into a unified knot.

The defectors that appear briefly in today's reading are very difficult to identify. You might open your Bible to 1 John and look up each of the references I am about to mention. One can spin a number of theories out of 2:19's statement that they were among the believers and then left, and then out of

2:22's statements about denying that Jesus is the Messiah, and then out of the disobedience statements about Jesus' commands (2:4–6), and then also out of 4:2's claim that some deny that Jesus was God incarnate. And maybe tie them all into the worldliness of 2:16. Many spin this into versions of early Christian heresies, like Gnosticism (or that matter is evil and other ideas) or Docetism (that Jesus only seemed to be fully human), or that some Jewish believers returned to the synagogue and denied Jesus was the Messiah. John, unlike many today, knows there is such a thing as religious truth. He also firmly knows that the embodied life of Jesus mattered and matters. He also knows that some who were among them have defected for the darkness, the un-life, and the life status climbing. John knows about true knowing.

To "Know" in 1 John

1 John 2:3–5 *We know that we have come to know him if we keep his commands. Whoever says, "I know him," but does not do what he commands is a liar, and the truth is not in that person. But if anyone obeys his word, love for God is truly made complete in them. This is how we know we are in him. . . .*

1 John 2:11 *But anyone who hates a brother or sister is in the darkness and walks around in the darkness. They do not know where they are going, because the darkness has blinded them.*

1 John 2:13–14 *I am writing to you, fathers,*
because you know him who is from the beginning.
I am writing to you, young men,
because you have overcome the evil one.
I write to you, dear children,
because you know the Father.
I write to you, fathers,
because you know him who is from the beginning.
I write to you, young men,
because you are strong,
and the word of God lives in you,
and you have overcome the evil one.

1 John 2:18 *Dear children, this is the last hour; and as you have heard that the antichrist is coming, even now many antichrists have come. This is how we know it is the last hour.*

1 John 2:20–21 *But you have an anointing from the Holy One, and all of you know the truth. I do not write to you because you do not know the truth, but because you do know it and because no lie comes from the truth.*

1 John 2:29 *If you know that he is righteous, you know that everyone who does what is right has been born of him.*

1 John 3:1–2 *See what great love the Father has lavished on us, that we should be called children of God! And that is what we are! The reason the world does not know us is that it did not know him. Dear friends, now we are children of God, and what we will be has not yet been made known. But we know that when Christ appears, we shall be like him, for we shall see him as he is.*

1 John 3:5 *But you know that he appeared so that he might take away our sins. And in him is no sin.*

1 John 3:10 *This is how we know who the children of God are and who the children of the devil are: Anyone who does not do what is right is not God's child, nor is anyone who does not love their brother and sister.*

1 John 3:14–15 *We know that we have passed from death to life, because we love each other. Anyone who does not love remains in death. Anyone who hates a brother or sister is a murderer, and you know that no murderer has eternal life residing in him.*

1 John 3:16 *This is how we know what love is: Jesus Christ laid down his life for us. And we ought to lay down our lives for our brothers and sisters.*

1 John 3:19–20 *This is how we know that we belong to the truth and how we set our hearts at rest in his presence: If our hearts condemn us, we know that God is greater than our hearts, and he knows everything.*

1 John 3:24 *The one who keeps God's commands lives in him, and he in them. And this is how we know that he lives in us: We know it by the Spirit he gave us.*

1 John 4:8 *Whoever does not love does not know God, because God is love.*

1 John 4:13 *This is how we know that we live in him and he in us: He has given us of his Spirit.*

1 John 4:16 *And so we know and rely on the love God has for us. God is love. Whoever lives in love lives in God, and God in them.*

1 John 5:2 *This is how we know that we love the children of God: by loving God and carrying out his commands.*

1 John 5:13 *I write these things to you who believe in the name of the Son of God so that you may know that you have eternal life.*

1 John 5:15 *And if we know that he hears us—whatever we ask—we know that we have what we asked of him.*

> **1 John 5:18–20** *We know that anyone born of God does not continue to sin; the One who was born of God keeps them safe, and the evil one cannot harm them. We know that we are children of God, and that the whole world is under the control of the evil one. We know also that the Son of God has come and has given us understanding, so that we may know him who is true. And we are in him who is true by being in his Son Jesus Christ. He is the true God and eternal life.*

ANTICHRIST

The term "antichrist" appears, as just mentioned, exactly five times in the entire New Testament. Three of them are in today's reading. But among many Bible readers today that term has become a fixed title for a single demonic person who will rule the world in the end—that is, according to one interpretation of the Bible's eschatology. For such a person, that singular figure is The Antichrist. This interpretation of antichrist (as The Antichrist) shapes the notes of many study Bibles; statements of faith in local churches; the sermons of scads of preachers; the lecture notes of professors; the books of authors, some of whom (like Hal Lindsay and Tim LaHaye) have become famous; and the instincts of millions of ordinary Christians. Again, a reminder: this term never appears in the book of Revelation.

So, let's back up and listen to what some informed

Christian thinkers say about this term. I begin with Anthony C. Thiselton, a New Testament specialist. He writes, "It is important to appreciate the contrast between the occasional occurrence of the word in the NT (only four references; note: actually there are five) and its more frequent occurrence in the Church Fathers and in Reformation and post-Reformation thought" (Thiselton, *The Thiselton Companion*, 26). Without saying so, his point is that the term *antichrist* took on a life of its own. David Hubbard, an Old Testament professor at Fuller Seminary and later president, adds some of the "life" this term acquired by speaking of those who believe in The Antichrist: "They believe that antichrist will usher in a period of great tribulation at history's close, in connection with a mighty empire like a revived Rome, dominating politics, religion, and commerce until Christ's advent. The temptation of identifying antichrist with the current figure periodically haunts such interpreters, distracting from clearer biblical teaching" (Hubbard, "Antichrist," 61). Such an interpretation usually identifies that singular Antichrist with one of the two beasts in Revelation's thirteenth chapter. The irony of this view weighs against that view because the very same author (John), who wrote about antichrists (not one antichrist), never identified either beast in Revelation with the term *antichrist*. Unfortunately, far too many have pounded a stake in the ground in identifying some world leader as the final Antichrist, and candidates have ranged from Nero to Putin, yet—pause for this—every one of the stakes had to be pulled up because the person pounding was wrong.

Kathleen Norris, once asked to speak to the women's circle at her church on the "Antichrist," asked her pastor for help. What he said might be helpful to hear today for many of us: "Each one of us acts as an Antichrist whenever we hear the gospel and do not do it" (Norris, *Amazing Grace*, 14–15). That might be extreme, but at least it balances out those who speculate endlessly and mistakenly about The Antichrist. Instead of this kind of speculation, I offer this challenge: nearly every one of those whom others identify as "The Antichrist" was a temporary expression of antichrist. So, yes, Nero and Hitler and Stalin. But let's not look for one. Let's exercise discernment with the help of God's Spirit to identify all those who opposed the way of God in this world in Christ as expressions of antichrist.

Here is what these five texts in John's letters say about the antichrist: (1) "the antichrist" is coming at the "last hour" but it seems that time zone is already in operation (2:18 and 2:8); (2) in fact, there is more than one antichrist, for John then says "even now many antichrists have come" (2:18); (3) John identifies those many antichrists as the defectors from the faithful in (probably) Ephesus (2:19); (4) "every spirit" that does not acknowledge that Jesus, God's Son, became a real human participates in "the spirit of the antichrist" (4:3); and (5) as such, that denier is a "deceiver and the antichrist" (2 John 7). John does not see the antichrist as a single supernatural figure at the end of history; John thinks of antichrists as those who deny the incarnation and the redemption that comes in Christ. Antichrist is a movement; it is the world. Having said that, John would see both beasts in Revelation, along with all the opponents of God's gospel, as antichrists.

So, this is what the Bible says: an antichrist is someone who opposes the truth of who Jesus is and what he has accomplished. Put differently, the label fits on far more people than need be counted. Having clarified this, however, we have a distinct problem: *We must be very cautious calling anyone today "antichrist" because the term itself has become a colossal figure at the end of time, a figure that is demonic, destructive, and death-dealing.* At times we might say someone is anti-Christian, but I would urge us to exercise more than extreme caution in labeling someone as antichrist today. Instead, we ought to proceed to John's way of dealing with the reality of defectors from the truth about Jesus Christ. That truth has been well-stated in the Nicene Creed, which reads:

> I believe in one Lord Jesus Christ, the Only Begotten Son of God, born of the Father before all ages. God from God, Light from Light, true God from true God, begotten, not made, consubstantial with the Father; through him all things were made.
>
> For us men and for our salvation he came down from heaven, and by the Holy Spirit was incarnate of the Virgin Mary, and became man. For our sake he was crucified under Pontius Pilate, he suffered death and was buried, and rose again on the third day in accordance with the Scriptures. He ascended into heaven and is seated at the right hand of the Father. He will come again in glory to judge the living and the dead and his kingdom will have no end. (See For Further Reading.)

That, or something close to it, is the truth about who Jesus is: God in the flesh, redeemer, Lord, judge, and future ruler of God's kingdom. The divisive, the schismatics, the disruptors of these basic truths about Jesus—these are those whom John calls antichrists.

Anointing

Karen Jobes asks a question that must have been circulating in the groups to which John sent this exhortation: "Who gets to speak for God?" (Jobes, *1–3 John*, 133). Evidently some in the community were saying "We do." John thinks one of the "we do" crowd are defectors, so the question becomes practical for him: What can prevent, or at least protect, believers from falling for bad ideas about Jesus and defecting? According to John, the answer is not "me" or "we do" but the "anointing." Anointing is another term in the Celtic knot, and it is a term that occurs only in 1 John, and this time only twice, and both in our passage (2:20, 27 [twice]). The term *chrisma* points at oil smeared or poured on a person. In a biblical sense, the one anointed is consecrated by God to be a priest, to rule as king, to be redeemed to a ministry or mission or to the destiny of Christoform transformation. It is possible that by the time John writes 1 John, a baptized person was anointed with oil. Which would suggest this term refers to a person's baptism. But that ought to remain on the shelf of suggestions.

The term, we should observe first, derives from the terms connected to "Christ," which is the Greek term for the Hebrew word "Messiah," which refers to "the anointed one." All to say that our *chrisma* participates in Christ's own *chrisma*. In addition, anointing and reception of the Spirit are connected in the Bible (Isaiah 61:1; Acts 10:38). Speaking of the Bible, some see the anointing as the Word of God abiding in us (cf. 1 John 1:1; 2:14; Ephesians 1:13). Others observe that what is said about the Spirit in today's reading connects as well with themes about the Paraclete/Spirit in John 14:17; 15:26; 16:13, and John says this anointing is from the "Holy One" (1 John 2:20). The themes are truth, remaining and indwelling, and knowing. First John's anointing, then, refers to the presence of Christ, the Word, and the Spirit in the believer (cf. 2 Corinthians 1:21–22). In both the Gospel of John and 1 John anointing refers to illumination about the truth of who Jesus is. The believers' anointing is followed immediately with "and all of you know the truth" (2:20). What they know they learned "from the beginning" and it indwells them, and this indwelling means they are indwelling the Son and the Father (2:24), and this anointed-indwelling leads to eternal life (2:25). Because there are defectors attempting to lead them astray, John points to the anointing as the sufficient teacher—they need not be led astray by false teachers. Even more, John writes that "his anointing teaches you about all things and as that anointing is real, not counterfeit—just as it has taught you, remain in him" (2:27). In short, remaining in Christ safeguards them and prevents defection.

Questions for Reflection and Application

1. What does John say about "antichrists"?

2. How has the concept of "The Antichrist" evolved from John's usage of "antichrists"?

3. Consider John's many words about "knowing." How would you summarize what he means by this term?

4. How can "anointing" protect those who are allegiant to Jesus from defecting from their faith?

5. In what ways has knowing truth protected you in your life?

FOR FURTHER READING

D. A. Hubbard, "Antichrist," in *Evangelical Dictionary of Theology*, 3rd ed.; eds. D. J. Treier, W. A. Elwell (Grand Rapids: BakerAcademic, 2017).

Nicene Creed: https://en.wikipedia.org/wiki/Nicene_Creed.

Kathleen Norris, *Amazing Grace: A Vocabulary of Faith* (New York: Riverhead, 1998).

A. C. Thiselton, *The Thiselton Companion to Christian Thought* (Grand Rapids: Wm. B. Eerdmans, 2015).

A NEW BIRTH
KIND OF LIFE

1 John 2:28–3:10

[28] *And now, dear children, continue in him, so that when he appears we may be confident and unashamed before him at his coming.*

[29] *If you know that he is righteous, you know that everyone who does what is right has been born of him.*

[3:1] *See what great love the Father has lavished on us, that we should be called children of God! And that is what we are! The reason the world does not know us is that it did not know him.* [2] *Dear friends, now we are children of God, and what we will be has not yet been made known. But we know that when Christ appears, we shall be like him, for we shall see him as he is.* [3] *All who have this hope in him purify themselves, just as he is pure.*

[4] *Everyone who sins breaks the law; in fact, sin is lawlessness.* [5] *But you know that he appeared so that he*

might take away our sins. And in him is no sin. ⁶No one who lives in him keeps on sinning. No one who continues to sin has either seen him or known him.

⁷Dear children, do not let anyone lead you astray. The one who does what is right is righteous, just as he is righteous. ⁸The one who does what is sinful is of the devil, because the devil has been sinning from the beginning. The reason the Son of God appeared was to destroy the devil's work. ⁹No one who is born of God will continue to sin, because God's seed remains in them; they cannot go on sinning, because they have been born of God. ¹⁰This is how we know who the children of God are and who the children of the devil are: Anyone who does not do what is right is not God's child, nor is anyone who does not love their brother and sister.

Children are identifiable because they talk like, act like, and often look like their parents and their siblings. The similarities are passed on to them by nature and nurture. Both of my children like reading and working—that's nurture. Both of them are Christians—God gets the credit for that one. Both of them are educated—it's a family value. Both like sports—no option there. Children truly have noticeable likenesses to their parents. Which leads us to what it means to be "children of God."

Spiritually we are shaped to be children of God by creation: we are in the image of God by (new) nature, in that the Spirit indwells us, and by nurture, in that we are formed by our faith community to be more like Jesus. Children of God are identifiable by how they live (or they should be). Karen Jobes lays out the alternatives for identifying whose children we are: "How one lives expresses whether one is born of God or of the devil" (Jobes, *1–3 John*, 137). We ought to remind people of Jesus the way folks in my hometown say to me, "You look so much like your father."

NEW BIRTH

The word "children" appears six times in today's reading. If we add "loved ones" (NIV: "friends"; 3:2) and the implied "God's child," which in Greek is only "from God" (*ek theou*; 3:10), the fuller picture can be seen. This passage, without once using the term, is about the new birth of the children of God. Sometimes the Bible refers to this as adoption (Romans 8:15, 23; 9:4; Galatians 4:5; Ephesians 1:5), at times as renewal (Titus 3:5), or a new birth. The reality these terms are speaking about is spiritual and supernatural. New birth transcends while transforming the material. In being born of God a person is given a new "heart" that beats according to God's heartbeat. To be "born of God" (1 John 2:28; 3:9–10), then, means a new birth, an idea found in John's Gospel (John 3:3, 7), in Paul (1 Corinthians 4:15; Galatians 4:29), in Peter (1 Peter 1:3, 23), but especially in 1 John (see sidebar: "New Birth in 1 John").

The essential idea is that the believer is spiritually reborn and given a new life. The idea is not just about birth because the terms used are connected as well to life. So, in *The Second Testament* I translate not "born of God" but "given life from

God" (3:9). The Greek term is *gennaō*, and the stem of this verb has the sense of a life given through reproduction. That is, to be born. But this birth is a divine, not human, birth, and it thus gives to a person a life from God, a life with God, and a life for God.

Our society, and especially the media, have reshaped the meaning of the term "evangelical" into "politically conservative and Republican" as well as "populist." In fact, many identify themselves in polls as "evangelical" and rarely ever participate in church—so much so that for such persons the term has a political meaning. But, when evangelicalism is defined by its core beliefs, at the bottom and at the beginning is a belief in the necessity of conversion, or new birth, to be a genuine Christian. David Bebbington has drafted the influential study on what "evangelical" means theologically, and he marks it with four terms, which unfortunately have had an unnecessary "ism" snapped on at the end: conversionism, biblicalism, crucicentrism, and activism. That is, the necessity of personal conversion to Jesus, the importance of the Bible for shaping beliefs, the centrality of the cross as the place of redemption, and activism in both evangelism and social justices (Bebbington, *Dominance*). The new birth, to be born of God, or to be converted then express the entrance code into a life of transformation into the image of Christ.

New Birth in 1 John

1 John 2:29 *If you know that he is righteous, you know that everyone who does what is right has been born of him.*

1 John 3:9 *No one who is born of God will continue to sin, because God's seed remains in them; they cannot go on sinning, because they have been born of God.*

1 John 4:7 *Dear friends, let us love one another, for love comes from God. Everyone who loves has been born of God and knows God.*

1 John 5:1 *Everyone who believes that Jesus is the Christ is born of God, and everyone who loves the father loves his child as well.*

1 John 5:4 *. . . for everyone born of God overcomes the world. This is the victory that has overcome the world, even our faith.*

1 John 5:18 *We know that anyone born of God does not continue to sin; the One who was born of God keeps them safe, and the evil one cannot harm them.*

For nearly forty years I have listened to the wonderful and worshipful music and lyrics of John Michael Talbot. My wife, Kris, and I have been to two of his conferences as well, and I have read a half dozen of his books. His newest, *Late Have I Loved You*, allows me one more time to walk with JMT through his life (and much of my own life). Though he opens with wondering about his "awareness at this late stage of my ministerial life that I have accomplished next to nothing in the eyes of the Lord" (5), he is also aware (and so are those like me to whom he has ministered over and over) that his influence has been redemptive. But I want to turn to the day he got his new life. He writes about it in this new memoir. He and his band, Mason Profitt, were climbing upward when he had an experience in a hotel room. He had begun praying for God to reveal himself. "Then one night, in some Midwest hotel room, the answer came. I looked up from my prayer and saw a light in the form of Christ. I knew it was Jesus. He didn't say anything. He didn't give me a great commission or a mission. . . . Christ was simply present, loving me with an indescribable love. . . . I also knew that all my sins were forgiven, and the sins of my rock 'n' roll lifestyle were beginning to stack up. I had strayed from the innocence and purity of my Christian youth and had left my faith altogether. In that moment, I knew it was time to come home. From that night on, I began to call myself a Christian again" (Talbot, *Late Have I Loved You*, 5, 28–29). That's the new birth about which Jesus and John talk. The rest of his story, which is a story of growing in Christlikeness, is for another day, but it all began when God granted John Michael Talbot a new life.

New birth evokes both something new and something from above (John 3:31; see 19:11), and it is only made possible by God's seed being implanted in us (1 John 3:8). We are given a new life through a new birth because God loves us (3:1). In fact, John says the Father's love is "great" and he has "lavished" it upon us. God enacts that new-life love for us by sending his Son, Jesus, to this world so he can destroy the "devil's work" (3:8). John does not enter into the expression of what we call Trinitarian theology. Instead of exploring *who God is* John concentrates on *what God does*, and the God of action for him is Father (referenced 12x), Son (22x in the NIV), and Spirit (6x).

This new birth leads to a new life of growth into Christlikeness, which is not fully complete until the final day. As we read, "All who have this hope in him [Christ and his return] purify themselves, just as he is pure" (3:3). Strikingly, John emphasizes the diminishment of sin, however gradual, however bumpy, and however forward and backward it may be. "No one," he writes, "who lives in him keeps on sinning" (3:6). That NIV rendering is not quite as blunt as John's own words, which are more like this: "Everyone who remains in him doesn't sin" (McKnight, *Second Testament*). John's blunt language continues with "Everyone who sins has not seen him and has not known him." He's not done yet, for in verse nine he writes, "Everyone who has been given life from God doesn't do sin" (*Second Testament*). God's children, since they have God's seed in them, the Spirit of God in them, and since they abide in Christ—because of these realities they are not sinners. Finally, the specific indicators of a new-birth kind of life are righteousness, or conformity to God's will, and love, which we defined previously (p. 73) (cf. 3:10).

The emphasis the NIV gives by adding the idea of continuing as a lifestyle accurately points us in the right direction. John knows Christians sin (1:5–2:2), but he also knows new birth creates a new-birth kind of life. His exaggerations are shaped to grab our attention, and I know he gets mine each time. The patterns of our life reveal whose children we are (3:7–8).

SIN

As mentioned immediately above, John knows believers sin and expects them to confess their sins to reenter into a fuller fellowship with God (1:9). In today's reading John returns to that opening passage about sin. He defines sin as breaking the law of Moses and intensifies sin by saying it is "lawlessness"— living outside the revealed will of God (3:4). This term is actually a very strong term (*anomia*), giving the sense of a reckless, rebellious disregard for the ways of God in Christ. *Anomia* borders on, if not crosses the line into, apostasy, especially as it pertains to the final great rebellion in apocalyptic literature (cf. 2 Thessalonians 2:3). It is a mistake to become preoccupied here with peccadillos Christians all commit, though there is no reason to flop over into casual disregard for holiness either. The sinless Son's very appearance was designed by God to remove "our sins" (3:5), which echoes 1:7, 9, and 2:1. If we reside in the sinless Son we ought to be the ones who "don't sin." In fact, sinful living denies our vision of Jesus and our knowing of Jesus (3:6). One has to wonder if

John's sense of "sin" in 3:4 pertains mainly, if not exclusively, to this sense of *anomia*, or reckless disregard of God's revelation in Christ. With that view of *anomia*, Thomas Bennett frames it like this: "To put it bluntly, there is a difference between sin and apocalyptic sin, between sinning and living completely without the light" (Bennett, *1–3 John*, 59).

Again, John ramps up his rhetoric to exhort the believers in Ephesus to turn toward Jesus Christ in surrendering trust and obedience in order to follow him more completely. He warns them of the dangers of wandering off the path to follow the defectors (2:18–27). Let's pause to notice how harsh John's words may seem to us, and let's ask why we sense them as harsh. It is very unlikely that the faithful follower of Jesus in John's day felt them as harsh. Rather, they had grown up with apostolic teaching that called believers to obedience and warned of the consequences of disobedience. Cheap grace has always been a temptation, and no doubt it was running rampant for some in John's churches, but John will have none of it. He calls them to a new-birth kind of life that abides in Christ in such a way that love and righteousness flourish in the life of a Christian. John's way of communicating the demand and cost of discipleship is a bold either-or: either your life is of the devil or your life is of Christ. The choice of following the defectors or the way of Christ makes his language much more understandable.

EXHORTATIONS

So his exhortations perfectly square with his message of a new-birth kind of life and the dangers of *anomia*. There is a give-and-return, a reciprocity in the new life. Months ago, Kris and I met a woman on our morning walk that has led to daily three- to five-minute conversations with her. One morning she came out with a gift of one of our favorite sweets: baklava. I will avoid whether Turkish or Greek baklava is the best, and I will avoid also where baklava was first created. (But it begins with a *T.*) The next weekend, when we stopped at our favorite bread store (Hewn), Kris said, "Let's buy our friend a fruit galette." Which we did. Now Kris and I exchange weekly gifts with our friend: baklava for a galette, a galette for baklava. That she gave us something prompted us to give something in return. Not to even the score, but to form a relationship of giving and receiving.

For John, God has given his Son and has provided redemption and transformation, and we are to express gratitude by giving God ourselves. In today's reading we discover the various responses of gratitude to God's giving: "continue in him" (2:28), doing what is "right" and thus not sinning and being purified (2:28, 29; 3:3, 4–6, 7, 8, 9, 10), and resist being led astray by false teachings (3:7). We can pause for a moment with each item.

First, we are to "remain" or abide in him. The image is of a residence in which one is residing, with the residing element taking on a life of its own. But we can ponder our relationship to Father, Son, and Spirit as one in which we reside, where we rest and find safety and nourishment and love and fellowship. As vines and branches reside in the root stalk and its roots, and so draws the sap that sustains it, so we are to reside in him (cf. 2:27, 28). By the way, John likes this term *menō,* or abiding and residing (see sidebar: "Abide/Reside in 1 John"). It's one of the terms at work in his Celtic knot of words. He uses the term eighteen times. To reside in the Father and the Son (2:24, 27, 28), or Christ, means to live as he did (2:6) and to follow his teachings (3:24) and to confess him (4:15); it means residing in the light (2:10); it means God (Father, Son, Spirit) as well as the Word of God and the "anointing" and God's seed residing in us (2:14, 27; 3:9; 3:24; 4:12, 13, 16); it means residing in a life that is eternal (2:17); it means residing in fellowship with the family of faith (2:19); it means not sinning (3:6); and it means to reside in love (4:16). This idea of residing means God in us and we in God—a living, interactive, reciprocal new-birth relational life of reception and giving (4:16). Our giving back to God, and our giving to one another, turns us from worldlings into children who look like God. To reside means to come to know and to remain in that knowing of God; to reside means knowing we are known by God.

Abide/Reside in 1 John

1 John 2:6 *Whoever claims to live in him must live as Jesus did.*

1 John 2:10 *Anyone who loves their brother and sister lives in the light, and there is nothing in them to make them stumble.*

1 John 2:14 *I write to you, dear children,*
because you know the Father.
I write to you, fathers,
because you know him who is from the beginning.
I write to you, young men,
because you are strong,
and the word of God lives in you,
and you have overcome the evil one.

1 John 2:17 *The world and its desires pass away, but whoever does the will of God lives forever.*

1 John 2:19 *They went out from us, but they did not really belong to us. For if they had belonged to us, they would have remained with us; but their going showed that none of them belonged to us.*

1 John 2:24 *As for you, see that what you have heard from the beginning remains in you. If it does, you also will remain in the Son and in the Father.*

1 John 2:27 *As for you, the anointing you received from him remains in you, and you do not need anyone to teach you. But as his anointing teaches you about all things and as that anointing is real, not counterfeit—just as it has taught you, remain in him.*

1 John 2:28 *And now, dear children, continue in him, so that when he appears we may be confident and unashamed before him at his coming.*

1 John 3:6 *No one who lives in him keeps on sinning. No one who continues to sin has either seen him or known him.*

1 John 3:9 *No one who is born of God will continue to sin, because God's seed remains in them; they cannot go on sinning, because they have been born of God.*

1 John 3:14–15 *We know that we have passed from death to life, because we love each other. Anyone who does not love remains in death. Anyone who hates a brother or sister is a murderer, and you know that no murderer has eternal life residing in him.*

1 John 3:17 *If anyone has material possessions and sees a brother or sister in need but has no pity on them, how can the love of God be in that person?*

1 John 3:24 *The one who keeps God's commands lives in him, and he in them. And this is how we know that he lives in us: We know it by the Spirit he gave us.*

1 John 4:12 *No one has ever seen God; but if we love one another, God lives in us and his love is made complete in us.*

1 John 4:13 *This is how we know that we live in him and he in us: He has given us of his Spirit.*

1 John 4:15–16 *If anyone acknowledges that Jesus is the Son of God, God lives in them and they in God. And so we know and rely on the love God has for us. God is love. Whoever lives in love lives in God, and God in them.*

Second, we are called to do what is right, and to do what is right means not sinning. Everything here depends on *knowing the standard* by which we measure what is right and what is sin. Righteousness in John's world describes a person whose behavior conforms to the standard being used. That standard is Christ, who is pure (3:3) and who teaches us (2:6) and whose image is so pure that we are destined to become like him and him alone (3:2). Many today use the standard of the American dream, or the American constitution, or "best practices" in the business world, or the law as articulated in our courts. None of which is the standard John used, and all of which are but glimpsing moments expressing something at work in the Christ-standard. To sin then is to behave in ways that break conformity to the Christ-standard. The Christ-standard is the only standard the follower of Jesus knows. The disciple of Jesus resides in Christ and so lives by the power of the Spirit in a way that conforms to that standard. John knows full conformity will only occur in the kingdom of God (3:3). Until then, we are on a journey of being conformed to Christ.

Third, John also teaches that residing in Christ empowers a person to resist false teachings. "Do not," he warns his readers, "let anyone lead you astray" (3:7). Or, as in *The Second Testament*, "let no one deceive you." John occasionally turns to the problems of deceit: "If we claim to be without sin, we deceive ourselves" (1:8), and he warns of those who are trying to deceive them (2:26; 3:7). The Spirit leads to truth but there is a spirit of deception, too (4:6). Connected to deception is lying. If we choose to walk in darkness while claiming to be in the light, we "lie" (1:6). Truth never lies (2:21), and the anointing all believers have blocks the lies, falsehood, and deception (2:27). The new-birth kind of life resides in God, and God in the person, and this mutual indwelling promotes Christoformity and residing in truth so fully we can recognize the lies of the evil one.

We are God's children. Children who talk like, act like, and look like Christ. We can recognize God's children only if and when we know God (Father, Son, Spirit). Those who know God know God's children. Those who recognize God in God's children know God.

QUESTIONS FOR REFLECTION AND APPLICATION

1. How does our creation in God's image, our new nature by the Spirit, and our nurture in Christian community shape us to look like children of God?

2. What are the dangers of focusing on little sins and neglecting the big picture of living in darkness and outside the light of Christ?

3. How do you put together the reality of sin in Christians and the words of John about not sinning?

4. Reflect on your conversion experience. What was it like for you when you experienced your new spiritual birth?

5. What aspects of your life cause the people around you to say, "You look like Jesus"?

FOR FURTHER READING

David Bebbington, *The Dominance of
    Evangelicalism: The Age of Spurgeon and Moody*
    (Downers Grove: IVP Academic, 2005).
For a summary of evangelicalism: https://
    en.wikipedia.org/wiki/Evangelicalism.
John Michael Talbot, *Late Have I Loved You:
    Recollections of a Life* (Berryville, Arkansas:
    Troubadour for the Lord Publishing, 2024).

LIVING IS LOVING

1 John 3:11–24

[11] *For this is the message you heard from the beginning: We should love one another. [12] Do not be like Cain, who belonged to the evil one and murdered his brother. And why did he murder him? Because his own actions were evil and his brother's were righteous. [13] Do not be surprised, my brothers and sisters, if the world hates you. [14] We know that we have passed from death to life, because we love each other. Anyone who does not love remains in death. [15] Anyone who hates a brother or sister is a murderer, and you know that no murderer has eternal life residing in him.*

[16] This is how we know what love is: Jesus Christ laid down his life for us. And we ought to lay down our lives for our brothers and sisters. [17] If anyone has material possessions and sees a brother or sister in need but has no pity on them, how can the love of God be in that person? [18] Dear children, let us not love with words or speech but with actions and in truth.

19 This is how we know that we belong to the truth and how we set our hearts at rest in his presence: 20 If our hearts condemn us, we know that God is greater than our hearts, and he knows everything. 21 Dear friends, if our hearts do not condemn us, we have confidence before God 22 and receive from him anything we ask, because we keep his commands and do what pleases him. 23 And this is his command: to believe in the name of his Son, Jesus Christ, and to love one another as he commanded us. 24 The one who keeps God's commands lives in him, and he in them. And this is how we know that he lives in us: We know it by the Spirit he gave us.

Just about every important term John uses in 1 John shows up in today's reading: love, world, life, love or hate, Jesus, loving others, truth, God, believing in Jesus, keeping God's commands, residing in God and God residing in us, and the Spirit. That's how John rolls. He circles back, he juts forward, adds a sidebar, responds to something he knows someone will ask, returns to where he was, says the same thing in a slightly different way. As we have said, it's like a Celtic knot. The unions between the terms are seamless and indetectable. What matters to John most is coming to terms with life, and for him to live is to learn to love God, self, and others. His favorite terms are actions and not abstractions. Love for him is a life that lives and dies for others; our hearts beat by loving; and the faith that we have morphs without disguise into following Jesus or obeying him.

John, more than all the apostles combined, has a pastor's heart. He knows many will respond exactly as many do today when they read his strong contrasts: Do I love enough? Am I walking in the light? For instance, we may be asking ourselves over and over in America's constant coverage of elections this question: *I really intensely and just about constantly dislike some current candidate for office. Does that make me a hater? Am I in the darkness?* As we reflect on this passage today, we will find John offering us realistic, pastoral consolation, especially in verses nineteen to twenty-four. The Bible does not demand or expect sinless perfection. John gets this exactly right: it expects us to live a life of love.

I cannot add this every time John calls us to love, but let it be said here for all the times it could be said: we are to know that a life of loving others does not coerce us to love sacrificially when it is unsafe for us sexually, physically, emotionally, and spiritually. The call and the yearning to love even our enemies does not require that we enter into relationships with those who will harm us. Even sacrificial love has its limits. Since John does not enter into that discussion, we will insert the observations here and let them linger with us as we learn about living love.

LIVING LOVE

When they turned their lives over to Jesus, at the very beginning of their formation, the new believers learned John's approach to the Christian life. It all begins with, it grows into, and it never ducks under, jumps over, or turns left or right from loving one another. Of course, this was the teaching of Jesus (John 13:34–35) and it was the Jesus Creed (Mark 12:28–34) and it was taught in the law of Moses (Deuteronomy 6:4–9; Leviticus 19:18), and we ought to see it going back to God's loving creation of the universe, but the instruction to be lovers of God and others was especially fresh and new with Jesus. For them it may have been utterly new when they learned about Jesus. To be a Christian is to be a person who loves God and loves others, and the latter reveals the former.

One influential approach to Christian living today directs one's life toward "spiritual formation." Bookshelves are filled with explanations and proposals and secrets to spiritual formation. No one has a one-and-done theory of how to live as a follower of Jesus. There is no secret sauce. Regardless of how it is framed—spiritual disciplines are in the middle of this discussion—for Jesus and for John what matters most is loving one another. Jesus planted so many seeds on the centrality of love that his teachings poke through the writings of his earliest followers (Galatians 5:14; Romans 13:8–10; 1 Corinthians 13; 1 Peter 1:22; 2:17; James 2:8–9). No one frames the one true life by love more than John, however. To live as God wants us to live is to love others. So, what is love?

> Love is a rugged, affective commitment to be with a person (presence) and to be for a person (advocacy) in order for both lover and beloved to grow together in virtue (direction), or Christlikeness or Christoformity.

The love test is to be asked if this is how we relate to others. End-of-the-day reflections can be approached with variations of one question: Did I love each person I encountered today? That is, Did I love God? Does my love for God reflect in my love for others? Does my love for others reflect God's love for me and for them?

Miguel Echevarría vulnerably reveals the challenge of loving others for persons of color in the American church today, where at times believers too often malign one another. I quote him: "We are sometimes taken aback when a person quotes doctrinal statements . . . but slander us for promoting racial reconciliation and social justice, accusing us of teaching critical theories or cultural Marxism. If they honestly evaluated our works, they would know that we are trying to obey Scripture's call to love our neighbor—which is the very thing John expects of us. Our social concern is rooted in the Bible, not secular teachings." He then offers words to other persons of color: "While it is difficult to love those who malign us, we must not succumb to hate" (Echevarría, "Letters," 715). Sometimes the most challenging acts of love are directed at our siblings in Christ.

As you now are aware, John likes bold, exaggerated contrasts. So, a life of love is posed against hating, and to give an example, he takes his listeners back to Genesis 4's story about Cain and Abel. Cain, Genesis 4 informs us, was downcast when his offering (vegetables, grains) was unfavorable to God. Abel's offering (fatty portions of the firstborn) was pleasing to God. YHWH asked Cain why he was "angry" (4:6) and revealed to Cain the challenge to live a good life:

"Sin is crouching at your door; it desires to have you, but you must rule over it" (4:7). The word of the Lord exposed the man's heart, and Cain failed the love test. Instead of admitting, confessing, and repenting, out of hatred Cain murdered his brother (4:8). Knowing all things, God asked Cain where his brother was, and Cain uttered words that have become plastic dismissal words: "Am I my brother's keeper?" (4:9). John reads the Cain and Abel story as the deep contrast of those who do "evil" and those who do what is right (1 John 3:12).

The "world," which we discussed at length previously in this study (pp. 43–53), frames for John those who do evil and who do not do what is right. As Cain's anger turned into hatred for his brother Abel, so the world hates those who do what is right. The indicator that a person is walking on the path of life, and away from the path of death, is loving one another (3:14). Those who, like Cain, choose hatred reside in the world of death. Hating a "brother or sister," John writes with perhaps a glance at the defectors, is a Cain-equivalent: a "murderer" (3:15). The dark-and-death path indicates that a person does not have "eternal life" residing in them. Love leads to life; hatred leads to death. Repetition with only slight variation describes the style of John.

DYING LOVE

Abel died; Cain killed him. The deepest irony of love immediately pops into John's quill. True love looks like Jesus' love, and Jesus "laid down his life for us" (3:16). True love does not murder; it dies for others. C. K. Barrett, full-time scholar and part-time Methodist preacher, observed that this verse (3:16) has a "we know" and "we ought," making it clear that what we know requires behaviors (our oughts) in line with what we know. It's the relationship of "knowledge and obligation" (Barrett, *Luminescence*, 2.316).

True life, then, ironically calls us to die for one another. True living is a dying love for one another. We can be easily tempted to turn this into sentimental idealism, into wearing a cross around our neck or getting a cross tattoo or purchasing a leather cover for our Bible with a cross on it. Dying love for John is immediately clarified with showing empathy for those in need: "Whoever has Kosmos's life and observes one's sibling having need and shuts one's empathies from the person—how does God's love remain in the person? Children, don't love in word or tongue but in work and truth" (3:17; *Second Testament*). In English, sympathy points to feeling for someone while empathy is about feeling with a person. In the latter, we enter into the other's emotions. We emote their emotions. The Greek term John uses is closer to empathy than sympathy. It is often translated with "pity" (NIV) or "compassion." The word is *splanchna* and refers to one's inner organs that are experienced as turning when we see someone in pain. The entire Bible teaches that God has empathy and we are to have empathy, and as God's empathy results in loving actions for us, so our empathy prompts us to do something for someone in need. But, with an important caveat: as Karen Jobes wisely reminds us, "God expects us to do what we can, not what we can't" (Jobes, *1–3 John*, 171).

Dying love dies to self in order to act for the other. But loving others can enter into some rugged seasons. What we think is loving for another may not be received well. What others may want from us as love may not be acceptable. But genuine love for others flows from a rugged, affective commitment of presence, mutuality, and direction, and that kind of commitment can involve dying to self. Whether that dying is a momentary choice not to do what we want or whether it is a lifetime decision to surrender our life for the good of others, the sense of dying at work is self-denial (Mark 8:34). Dying love then is not reducible to the feeling of empathy, sympathy, pity, or compassion; dying love allows those feelings to morph into actions (3:18). But hear this: Love cannot be reduced to actions. Love is a feeling-generated action of good for another. Rabbi Shai Held has had a mission to correct Christian misperceptions of Judaism's central teachings. In particular, he wants Christians to know that their Bible and his (the Christian Old Testament) teaches the centrality of love (e.g., Deuteronomy 6:4–9; Leviticus 19:18). In teaching this, Held emphasizes love as both emotion and action. Here is one of his oft-repeated ways of holding both in his hand: love is "an existential posture, a life orientation, a way of holding ourselves in the world; it's a way of life." He continues: "What I mean when I speak of love as an existential posture or a life orientation is, in part, that it is a disposition to feel certain things and act in certain ways" (Held, *Judaism Is About Love*, 9). He, too, knows that true love dies to self for the good of another, not as a way of diminishing our integrity or degrading our self-identity but as a choice to do good to the other. His study of the Bible leads him to a theology of love that is very much like a Christian approach to love: God loves us; this makes us valuable; we are grateful for God's love; gratitude prompts reciprocal love on our part—we love God back and we love others.

So, in asking how we measure according to the standard of love, we can't ask simply how we feel about others. We need also to ask what we do that indicates our love for the other person. We can then learn to identify what emotions are percolating in us as we act for that other person. We may discover that in acting kindly toward someone, emotions of empathy and love are turned on inside us. In living love we learn that love is dying, and we also learn that our deepest inner world comes alive, and that inner world is called the heart by John.

LOVING HEARTS

We could expect John to say that "we know that we belong to the truth" because we act in love toward others. That would be very Johannine. But 3:19 does not go there. Instead, we read this: "This is how we know that we belong to the truth and how we set our hearts at rest in his presence." I tell my students all the time that what is most needed for a writing life is tranquility. Those who write often will know that prayer and writing are very similar exercises. Having enough rest in our hearts to put words onto paper approximates putting words and even silence before God in prayer. In attempting to be silent we will know whether tranquility is present or not. Mindy Caliguire writes, "In the cacophony of life's demands and pressures"—hold her sentence right there: don't we all know this all too frequently?—she continues with "God invites us to still and quiet our souls." And she quotes that amazing line in Psalm 46:10: "Be still, and know that I am God." Mindy describes a retreat she once arranged. Of the four hours she was at the location for her retreat, she found only fifteen minutes of attentive stillness of soul (Caliguire, *Ignite*, 119). Knowing our hearts, which only comes through times of attentive stillness, is both an achievable and a needed knowing.

We tend to think of our heart as a metaphor for our emotions and feelings, which it is. But it is more. It is both emotions and mind, emotions and will, emotions and agency. Heart refers to the fully engaged self. The biblical picture of a human, and the heart stands for the whole person, is a person who is both self-aware and self-engaged emotionally, rationally, and volitionally. Jesus taught us to love God and others as ourselves in the heart, soul, mind, and strength (Mark 12:30). But these separable terms are not distinct parts of a human. Rather, each expresses differing ways to look at a whole loving human being.

What follows is whether or not our "heart" is "knowably wrong" (3:20–21; *Second Testament*). The NIV translates with "condemn." The Greek word combines *knowing* with *against* (*kataginōskō*). We are not to think of God condemning or judging, which translates a different Greek term (*katakrinō*), but of the inner voice approving or not approving. John basically presses his discussion into our own life by asking us to interrogate ourselves with this question: *What is my heart saying about what and how I am doing?* Because God indwells us, because God's seed is in us, because we are in God, John trusts that the heart knows its condition. Even if our heart knows we're wrong, God's grace encompasses us (3:20). When our heart knows we are not knowingly wrong in how we are living, we discover an inner assurance and confidence in approaching God. In approaching God with a heart not knowingly wrong, we also discover answered prayer requests (3:21–22).

Speaking of our inner voice can cause confusion. Some inner voices have become captured by a scrupulosity and perfectionism that say to us, "You are bad" and "You are wrong" and "You are unworthy of love"—all the time, or far too often. Some inner voices have been captured by narcissism and selfishness that say, "You are good" and "You are right"—all the time, or far too often. A Spirit-drenched, Word-shaped, God-formed inner voice informs us of sin and affirms our goodness, and it informs us of what is evil and affirms what is true. Conforming our inner voice to the voice of God's good love for us can take healing, sometimes through some painful seasons, but God has sent the Spirit to us for our healing.

OBEYING FAITH

Another surprise from John, but not surprising if we recall how today's reflection began. Just about everything John writes in 1 John shows up as John weaves and bobs through his favorite themes: love, world, life, love or hate, Jesus, loving others, truth, God, believing in Jesus, keeping God's commands, residing in God and God residing in us, and the Spirit. Well, even if we know his style we can be surprised what happens when he moves from our inner voice to prayer requests to believing.

In particular, instead of language about the heart following "we have confidence before God" (3:21), John moves into prayer requests being answered and to obeying the teachings of Jesus and doing what pleases him (3:22). I know I didn't expect that. Then another surprise: from doing the will of God John guides us to see the will of God in this: "to believe in the name of his Son, Jesus Christ" (3:23). Which leads to a few non-surprises: following faith in Christ we are "to love one another as he commanded us," and obeying Jesus means residing in God and God in us, and to knowing God lives in us because we know we have the Spirit, which takes us right back to the heart (3:24). If that is a bit knotted together, that's exactly how John progresses and hops from one theme to another. His favorite themes are all connected: God loves us; we are called to love God; if we love God, we live in the light and we have life and we love one another, and the world doesn't like those who love God and live in the light and so pursue eternal life.

Eugene Peterson tells a beautiful story I will summarize. Once on a pastoral visit, the woman he was visiting had gone to the kitchen to get some coffee so he peered into the impressive trophy display that belonged to her husband. When she returned, he observed how good her husband must have been. She responded with, "He is very good. Why, it's his second love." Which of course led Peterson to ask what his first love was, and she said in no uncertain terms, "Me." She knew where she stood, he wrote, in "a highly competitive world." Peterson does not take this to ethics; he takes us to theology. He doesn't grind us down to ask who is first in our love. He reminds us that "God has made it clear that in fact you are first place" in the divine heart of love (Peterson, *Lights a Lovely Mile*, 172–173). First John 3:1 and 3:16 are the places to start for today's reading: God has loved us with an immeasurable love in sending his Son for us. It's how we know what love is.

QUESTIONS FOR REFLECTION AND APPLICATION

1. In what ways do you see John's pastoral heart show up in his writing?

2. What are some important limits to sacrificial love that McKnight points out in this section?

3. What does a life of love look like to John?

4. How does John's use of empathy/compassion and action-oriented love impact your understanding of what it means to live an others-loving life?

5. When you pay attention to your inner voice, what do you notice about it? Is it shaped by the Spirit or shaped by the world?

FOR FURTHER READING

C. K. Barrett, *Luminescence: The Sermons of C. K. and Fred Barrett*, volume 2, ed. Bem Witherington III (Eugene, Oregon: Cascade, 2017).

Mindy Caliguire, with Shawn Smucker, *Ignite Your Soul: When Exhaustion, Isolation, and Burnout Light a Path to Flourishing* (Colorado Springs: NavPress, 2024).

Shai Held, *Judaism Is About Love: Recovering the Heart of Jewish Life* (New York: Farrar, Straus and Giroux, 2024).

Eugene Peterson, *Lights a Lovely Mile: Collected Sermons of the Church Year* (Colorado Springs: WaterBrook, 2023).

OVERCOMING HERESIES IN THIS LIFE

1 John 4:1–6

[1] *Dear friends, do not believe every spirit, but test the spirits to see whether they are from God, because many false prophets have gone out into the world.* [2] *This is how you can recognize the Spirit of God: Every spirit that acknowledges that Jesus Christ has come in the flesh is from God,* [3] *but every spirit that does not acknowledge Jesus is not from God. This is the spirit of the antichrist, which you have heard is coming and even now is already in the world.*

[4] *You, dear children, are from God and have overcome them, because the one who is in you is greater than the one who is in the world.* [5] *They are from the world and therefore speak from the viewpoint of the world, and the world listens to them.* [6] *We are from God, and whoever knows God listens to us; but whoever is not from God does not listen to us. This is how we recognize the Spirit of truth and the spirit of falsehood.*

A friend of mine once described working at a bank for a couple years. He then proceeded to talk about his first few days at the bank, and now my memory is only as reliable as the gist of what happened. For the first day he was given bundles of dollar bills and told to count each one into a pile, touching them, pulling one from the pile, and making another pile. Over and over and over he counted dollar bills. Until he *knew what they felt like*. But he was not done. If my memory is right, he was sent into a room to do this several times the first week to touch, feel, and count dollar bills *until he could recognize counterfeit bills*, which his director had inserted into some of the stacks of bills.

I don't remember that my friend was talking about our passage, but he could have been. The connection I'm making is this: the only way to know false spirits and antichrists (see p. 104) is to know the Spirit and the Christ. The more we know the Christ, the more we can discern the antichrists. To know the truth means knowing falsehoods. To know love is to know hate. To know the church is to know the world. To know the truth is to know heresy. John provides for us in today's reading a safe process for recognizing heresies and heretics. Calling out a heresy, and even more naming someone a "heretic," are very serious actions and ought to be done (1) only by those who know the truth and (2) only after serious conversations about what the person teaches. In fact, in the history of the church only teachers in the church who had been warned, investigated, and given time to respond and repent—and all under pastoral care—could be called out for heresy. Yet, heresy and heretics happen. What can we learn from John about this?

We Can Learn to
Test the Spirits

We are invited by John (1) not to "believe every spirit" but (2) to "test the spirits" and to do this (3) "to see whether [the spirits] are from God" (4:1). This is a proper *healthy suspicion*. If we have done our duty to understand Christian truth, which begins with the Bible and the classic creeds of the church (see p. 64), and if we hear something both new and strange, we have an obligation to ask questions with a healthy suspicion. We don't need to be pushy or aggressively suspicious, and we must avoid being mean-spirited. We are to choose the spirit of inquiry. Noticeably, the testing of the spirits arises because "many false prophets" can be encountered.

A healthy suspicion leads us to test the spirits, that is, to approve what is truthful and disapprove of what is false. This term "spirits" deserves some attention. Both the Old and New Testaments have a standard term that is often translated with "spirit." The Hebrew term is *ruach* and the Greek term is *pneuma*. Either can refer to wind, to air, to God's Spirit, to a human spirit, to angels, and to an evil spirit or demon. In our context the spirits in need of testing are known from what humans are saying. Thomas Bennett points us in the right direction when he writes that the spirits are "spiritual beings whose influence manifests itself in human life" (Bennett, *1–3 John*, 71). That is, he has in mind the general sense of the spirit at work in a person that reveals whether or not they are walking in the light, in the life of God, and in the truth. Yet, since John operates with a strong either-or, with light vs.

darkness, with truth vs. the lie, we have every reason to think a spirit that is not in line with the truth is an evil spirit. If we widen our scope, we could easily think John has in mind what he calls Babylon in Revelation 17–18. Not every word of a gifted person in Christ who is indwelt by the Holy Spirit is of God. Each of us fails to discern the truth. A healthy suspicion, because it asks questions, can prompt deeper perceptions of the truth, can reveal error and even false teachings.

For John's context, which is not the same as ours, the fundamental starting point in this testing of spirits is if the person confesses that "Jesus Christ has come in the flesh" (4:2). Those who are "of God" publicly acknowledge that truth. False spirits deny that confession. Those who deny the truth about Jesus Christ reveal the "spirit of the antichrist" (4:3). In John's day, this antichrist-spirit had already begun its work—and that can only mean it is more pervasive today than it was then. Many will feel the challenge of testing while others will back away because they wonder if they have the gifts and experience for testing the spirits. While each believer is called to confess the truth about Jesus Christ, knowing sufficient theology to discern the realities of falsehoods is not for everyone. However, John blocks the path of despair. He comforts us by reminding us that we are overcomers.

We have an obligation to test the spirits. Truth matters. Confusion accompanies us on the path. The gospel matters. Confession that Jesus is the Messiah matters. Truth cuts deep divisions between those who affirm truth and those who deny the truth. There are counterfeit "Christians" in our world as much as there were in John's. There are those who claim to believe the truth but don't. There are those who teach the truth but deny it privately or by the way they live. Professing believers can lead others astray. At times we may feel some idea or person is off and not be able to name it clearly; at other times, we can do both, and we will need to name it appropriately. Confessing Christ and denying a life of discipleship and transformation needs to be named. Claiming to be a follower of Jesus and living in the world needs to be seen as hypocrisy. Choosing with whom we fellowship will both embody our confession and shape our discipleship, so we need to choose wisely (especially for our children's sake). The deepest truths here are whether or not Jesus is truly Lord and if we square our life with that truth. That deep truth prompts the deep question: Who do you think Jesus was and is? One's answer reveals where one is. Jesus-centeredness is the ultimate matter. As C. K. Barrett once summed it all up: "God centered, Christ centered, love centered" (C. K. Barrett, *Luminescence* 2.323).

WE CAN LEARN THAT
WE HAVE OVERCOME

"You," he says immediately, are not only [1] "from God" but you [2] "have overcome" the spirits that are antichrist. The power to overcome derives not from our intelligence, our theology, our education, or our skills to persuade. The power to overcome is "because the one who is in you is greater than the one who is in the world" (4:4). The "one who is in you" is God—Father, Son, Spirit. I prefer to translate that first "one" with "One." The second "one" remains lowercase because it is the spirit of antichrist. Those spirits are "from the world" (see p. 45–49). In addition to what is written above about the world, we observe that the world is used in three ways in the New Testament:

1. As a place or location, that is, as God's creation (Acts 17:24)
2. As a moment in time (Hebrews 4:3), as the time for choosing God (James 2:5; Hebrews 11:38)
3. As an agent at war with God (James 4:4; 1 John 3:13; 5:19; B. J. Dodd, "World")

We might accuse John of having more than a healthy suspicion of the spirits, but John knows what this world is made of, and he has such a firm grip on the truth of the gospel that he spots the spirit of antichrist and worldliness with more depth than most. He knows the dangers. He can feel the counterfeit. Worldlings understand worldliness. In fact, the spirits of the world understand only what is of the world.

"We are from God" and they are "from the world." This splitting of all humans into two groups immediately leads us to come to terms with the importance of our community. Those "from God" know the truth and they know one another and they confess the truth, and they do this in contrast to the worldlings of this world. We can "recognize the Spirit of truth" over against the "spirit of falsehood" by discerning who it is that listens to us and who it is that doesn't listen to us. John's sense of community is not the denominationalism of our day where Baptists and Presbyterians and

Anglicans battle with one another, even though in generous moments they recognize we are one in Christ. No, John's division is between the spirit of antichrist and the Spirit of God, between those who confess Jesus has come in the flesh and those who deny that truth.

Confessing the true life of God in Christ and in the Spirit locates a person "in" God, but also, we need to see the mutual opposite: God (Father, Son, Spirit) "in" the person. With God for us, with us, and in us, we can overcome the temptations to deny Christ, to return to the world, to follow the spirits of antichrist, and to indulge in the "lust of the flesh, the lust of the eyes, and the pride of life" (2:16). Overcoming does involve discerning and testing, but the power to overcome derives from God in us.

QUESTIONS FOR REFLECTION AND APPLICATION

1. How does knowing the truth intimately help us discern untruths?

2. What are some hallmarks of a healthy suspicion?

3. How is the phrase "the world" used in the New Testament?

4. Why is it so important to choose carefully the people with whom we are in close relationship?

5. What help do you need from God today to overcome the world in your life?

FOR FURTHER READING

C. K. Barrett, *Luminescence: The Sermons of C. K. and Fred Barrett*, volume 2, ed. Bem Witherington III (Eugene, Oregon: Cascade, 2017).

B. J. Dodd, "World," in *The Dictionary of the Later New Testament and Its Developments*, ed. R.P. Martin, P.H. Davids (Downers Grove: IVP,1997), 1222–1224.

TEN ELEMENTS OF
THE LOVE LIFE

1 John 4:7–21

(emphasis added)

*⁷ Dear friends, let us **love** one another, for **love** comes from God. Everyone who **loves** has been born of God and knows God. ⁸ Whoever does not **love** does not know God, because God is **love**. ⁹ This is how God showed his **love** among us: He sent his one and only Son into the world that <u>we</u> might live through him. ¹⁰ This is **love**: not that we **loved** God, but that he **loved** <u>us</u> and sent his Son as an atoning sacrifice for <u>our</u> sins. ¹¹ Dear friends, since God so **loved** <u>us</u>, we also ought to **love** one another. ¹² No one has ever seen God; but if we **love** one another, God lives in <u>us</u> and his **love** is made complete in <u>us</u>.*

¹³ This is how we know that <u>we</u> live in him and he in <u>us</u>: He has given <u>us</u> of his Spirit. ¹⁴ And we have seen and testify that the Father has sent his Son to be the Savior of the world. ¹⁵ If anyone acknowledges that Jesus

is the Son of God, God lives in them and they in God.[16]
And so we know and rely on the **love** *God has for* <u>*us*</u>.

God is **love**. *Whoever lives in* **love** *lives in God, and
God in them.* [17] *This is how* **love** *is made complete among*
<u>*us*</u> *so that we will have confidence on the day of judgment:
In this world we are like Jesus.* [18] *There is no fear in* **love**.
But perfect **love** *drives out fear, because fear has to do with
punishment. The one who fears is not made perfect in* **love**.

[19] *We* **love** *because he first* **loved** <u>*us*</u>. [20] *Whoever
claims to* **love** *God yet hates a brother or sister is a liar.
For whoever does not* **love** *their brother and sister, whom
they have seen, cannot* **love** *God, whom they have not
seen.* [21] *And he has given us this command: Anyone who*
loves *God must also* **love** *their brother and sister.*

Count the words in bold in today's reading. My tally is twenty-seven. Three times more than the number of times love appears in 1 Corinthians 13, the so-called love chapter. And I didn't even count the "Dear friends" where the word "friends" translates *agapētoi*, or "loved ones." So, make it twenty-nine. John not only outran Peter to the tomb (John 20:4), he has outrun Paul when it comes to love. Today's reading deserves to be called the Love Portion of the Bible. (Not "love potion"!) What do we learn about love in this newly named Love Chapter? At least ten elements are at work in today's reading. I will approach the passage by topic instead of by verses—to avoid John's (forgive me for saying this) repetitions. Patrick Mitchel, who has written the best study about love in the Bible that I have read, states an important reality that alone can help us make sense of today's passage: we are "first and foremost lovers. It is not a question of *whether* we will love; it is *what* we will love" (Mitchel, *The Message of Love*, 116). Humans are designed by God to love. The family relationships that form in Christ are relationships for lovers of one another, and of God.

#1: GOD IS LOVE

Love, as we have defined in the Everyday Bible Study series, is a rugged, affective commitment to be with a person (presence) and to be for a person (advocacy) in order for both lover and beloved to grow together in virtue (direction), or Christlikeness or Christoformity. What happens to this definition when we look at God's love?

> God's love is a rugged, affective commitment to be with us (presence) and for us (advocacy) that transforms us into those who grow in loving a relational, interactive God as God loves (direction). That direction is Christlike and transforms us into Christlikeness in our love.

But John goes deeper. It is not just that God loves but that God *is* love (4:8, 16). Theologians are quick to add that this is a non-reciprocating statement. God is love does not mean all forms of love are God. To say love is God turns something (love) into God, which is idolatry. No, God's being, who God is, and therefore all that God does, is love. God cannot *not* love because God *is* love. If God were not to love, God would cease being God. God is love is not a Christian invention. Moses, after smashing the first edition of the Ten

115

Commandments, meets with God, who gives him a second edition. At this moment God defines himself in these terms:

> The LORD, the LORD, the compassionate and gracious God, slow to anger, abounding in love and faithfulness, maintaining love to thousands, and forgiving wickedness, rebellion and sin. (Exodus 34:6–7)

As the God who *is* compassionate and gracious and slow to anger and abounding in love and faithfulness, and who maintains that love endlessly, this God therefore forgives sinners of their idolatries and sins. John's God "is" love then is a refreshing restatement of Moses. We may go back-and-forth with "God is good" followed by "all the time," but the deeper truth is that God is love all the time. Because God is love, God is good.

You may wonder how Exodus 34:7's expressions of God's anger that follow on from God's love fit together. Many have discussed this. The best discussions conclude that God *is* love and *because* God is love, God cannot tolerate sin and idolatries. Anger is what God *does*, not who God *is*. Anger is God's holy response to what defies who God is. "God gets angry," as Shai Held has said, "because God cares" (Held, *Judaism Is About Love*, 285).

#2: GOD'S LOVE IS PRIOR TO ALL LOVE

The Creator is love, and since the Creator is prior to the entire universe, God's love is prior to our love of God and our love of others. In that sense, we cannot take credit even for our growth in loving God, loving self, and loving others. God's love is the air we breathe; without that air we cannot breathe. Love is "from" and "of" God (4:7). Love is God-likeness.

Even skimpy, superficial acts of love, however inadequate and unsatisfying, come from God. To be sure, some of what is said about love on the music scene, from John Lennon to Taylor Swift, falls short of John's teachings about love. Yet, if God is love then all love we know has its origins in the God of love. Even the distortions of love point to the ultimacy of love in God who reveals true love in Jesus Christ.

John was quick to put us in our place when it comes to love. Love is "not that we loved God" but that God first "loved us" (4:10). We can only love because God "lives in us," and because God is absolutely complete, our love can only be completed—in loving God, loving self, and loving others—because of the completeness of God (4:12). So, John repeats and sums it all up in verse nineteen: "We love because he first loved us."

#3: God Loves Us

John wants his readers to know that God loves them. We might want to read today's passage all over again and mark the words "we" and "us." I'm thinking now especially of the *us* in verses nine, ten, eleven, twelve, thirteen, sixteen, seventeen, nineteen, and twenty-one. (I underlined them in today's reading.) It would not take much effort on our part to find other uses of *us*, *we*, or *our*. Over and over we hear the voice of John who is but an echo of God's own voice in his Son through the Spirit: God has his eye on us, God loves us, and God's love—again—is

117

. . . a rugged, affective commitment to be with us (presence) and for us (advocacy) that transforms us into those who grow in loving a relational, interactive God as God loves (direction). That direction is Christlike and transforms us into Christlikeness in our love.

God is not just hanging out with us. God's love is a gracious act of coming to us so we can be reborn into an interactive relationship with the Creator-God. God's love is redemptive and transformative all at once. The more we live in God's love the more Christlike we become.

You may need to pause. Many of us, for all sorts of reasons and experiences in our past, do not easily receive God's love. But God's love is coming for you because it has always come for you, it is coming for you now, and it will continue to come for you forever and ever. You can run but God is faster; you can hide but God can see you. He wants you to know love. We cannot face God without knowing the God who *is* love. The only God that exists is the God who is love. The God who is love is the God who comes for you and for me. Please face this God in the face of Jesus and see God for who God truly is: love.

#4: JESUS EMBODIES AND REVEALS GOD'S REDEMPTIVE LOVE

The God who is love reveals himself, which means he reveals love, in sending his Son, Jesus Christ, to redeem us. We know

God because we know Jesus. Apart from Jesus we cannot know the fullness of who God is. The Jesus we know is the Jesus who lived, who taught, who did miracles, who loved his own, who died for us, who was raised for us, who ascended for us, and who will come for us. This Jesus reveals God. Those who imagine or envision God apart from the Man from Galilee cannot know God in truth. God "showed his love among us" by sending his Son so "we might live through him" (4:9). This, John says, is love: "that God loved us and sent his Son as an atoning sacrifice for our sins" (4:10). God's love for us and God's redemption of us in Christ are the flipsides of the Love Song.

When John, searching perhaps for the words to say the same thing with a little freshness, summarizes complete love for us he writes, "In this world we are like Jesus" (4:17). Not only does God reveal the depths of divine love in sending his Son, but we are summoned to a love that looks like God's love in Jesus and Jesus' life as a life of love. The Greek is less explicit than the NIV's translation. *The Second Testament* illustrates the Greek's indirection with "because just as he is so also we are in this Kosmos." That "he is" with the "so also" takes on new shape in the NIV, but the new shape is true to the sense. What God's love is (Jesus Christ) so our love is to be (Jesus-like).

#5: LOVING GOD MEANS KNOWING GOD, AND KNOWING GOD REQUIRES LOVING GOD

We are reminded that loving is a kind of knowing. To love God or to love another person is to come to know God or the other person. Because all love ultimately comes from God, John can say "everyone who loves" has not only "been born of God" but also "knows God" (4:7b). N. T. Wright has written that "real knowledge isn't your knowledge of the world or God, but God's knowledge of you. Your answer to that 'knowledge' is first and foremost love, because the revelation is itself love" (Wright, *History and Eschatology*, 207). Since all knowing is relational, only the deepest of relations—love—knows fully. Long ago J. I. Packer expounded the difference between knowledge *about* God and knowledge *of* God. In pondering how we can make the transition from "about" to "of," he wrote, "The rule for doing this is simple but demanding. It is that we turn each truth that we learn *about* God into matter for meditation *before* God, leading to prayer and praise *to* God" (Packer, *Knowing God*, 23).

John teaches us where to begin: by knowing God in Jesus Christ. To know God is to be known by God. To know God is to know Jesus Christ and to be known by Jesus Christ. To know Jesus Christ is to know Jesus loves you and to love Jesus.

#6: ALL TRUE LOVE EXTENDS GOD'S LOVE

A brief reminder about this sixth element, and this element restates the second element above. If God is love, all love comes from God. Which means when we love one another we are only extending God's love—for creation, for us, for the siblings in Christ—to others. "Everyone," John says, "who loves," and by this he means genuine love made complete by the Spirit (see element #7), "has been born of God and knows God" (4:7b). Our love flows from God's love. There is no source of love other than God.

#7: GOD'S LOVE OF US PROMPTS OUR LOVE OF OTHERS

The seventh element, too, expands on and extends elements two and six. In today's reading the most repeated theme is that God, as the only source of love, generates love in us for others. Love comes "from God" (4:7). God's love in Christ prompts our love for one another (4:11). When we recognize that we love one another, we also recognize we love because "God lives in us" and it is his love that is "made complete in us" (4:12). Thomas Slater calls this "theological genetics" (Slater, "1–3 John," 538). Divine DNA has been implanted in us that both makes it possible for us to become lovers and empowers us to reach out in love to others.

In the only paragraph in today's reading without the term "love" until the very last line, John somehow manages to talk about love without using the term (until that last line). I'm referring to 4:13–16a. God's living in us is followed to its origins: God "has given us of his Spirit" (4:13). The Spirit in us leads us to "testify that the Father has sent the Son to be the Savior of the world" (4:14), leading John to circle back to God in us. This time, however, by claiming that confession that Jesus, God's royal Son, means "God lives in [us] and [we] in God" (4:15). If we trace this circular path, we come to love: "And so we know and rely on the love God has for us" (4:16). The love God has for us is "made complete among us" when we live "like Jesus" (4:17).

I have done my best to follow the path, and we discover it is a circle, or a Celtic knot. Love comes from God, enters into us through Christ and in the Spirit, and this God-in-reality of knowing God prompts us to become those who love others, which is the eighth element of love in today's reading.

#8: Love of God Requires Loving One Another

To know God is to love God; to love God is to know God. True knowing and loving of God requires us to love one another. Patrick Mitchel writes that John has no patience for "cheap love, where we say we love God but do not act accordingly" (Mitchel, *The Message of Love*, 116). John has his eye on the church and on the defectors. Those, he says, who don't love their in-Christ siblings "cannot love God" (4:20). We are a family of lovers. Families love one another. If someone opts to leave the family, one does not love the family. Loving the family requires remaining in fellowship with one another. Loving God means loving God's people. In fact, this is a "command" (4:21), an obligation, and an "ought" (4:11). To love as Christ loved is to give ourselves for another, to sacrifice ourselves for the other.

One of the harshest realities of the church has been

puritanical attempts to purify the church. There is no reason to think the church should not be criticized for coercive puritanical moves. After all, Paul takes on churches with the severest of expressions. Dietrich Bonhoeffer's words spur me to these thoughts as a commentary on John's words:

> Christian community means community through Jesus Christ and in Jesus Christ. There is no Christian community that is more than this, and none that is less than this. (Bonhoeffer, *Life Together*, 31)

If we are in Christ, we cannot get away from the church, or the community of Jesus. All who are in Christ are there with us. Yet, many want more than the simple fellowship of one another in Christ.

> Those who want more than what Christ has established between us do not want Christian community. They are looking for some extraordinary experiences of community that were denied them elsewhere. Such people are bringing confused and tainted desires into the Christian community. Precisely at this point Christian community is most often threatened from the very outset by the greatest danger, the danger of internal poisoning, the danger of confusing Christian community with some wishful image of pious community, the danger of blending the devout hearts natural desire for community with the spiritual reality of Christian community. (Bonhoeffer, *Life Together*, 34–35)

His oft-quoted words follow shortly after the above:

> Every human idealized image that is brought into the Christian community is a hindrance to genuine community and must be broken up so that genuine community can survive. Those who love their dream of a Christian community more than the Christian community itself become destroyers of that community even though their personal intentions may be ever so honest, earnest, and sacrificial. . . . The bright day of Christian community dawns wherever the early morning mists of dreamy visions are lifting. (Bonhoeffer, *Life Together*, 36, 37)

One more: "Christian community is not an ideal we have to realize, but rather a reality created by God in Christ in which we may participate" (Bonhoeffer, *Life Together*, 38). False forms of reconciliation, forced demands of restitution, and faked confessions flow from the ideals we bring into the church. Furthermore, added requirements have become the norm for far too many churches. What constitutes fellowship is not enlightened ideas or theological refinements but the Spirit of God in us. All that is needed is Christ; more than what Christ has constituted burdens the church. Added elements distort the ground of our fellowship.

In Christ we are family, and families are not perfect forms of fellowship. What unites us is the life we have in Christ, not the light we perceive in our theology. These words of Bonhoeffer's take us to the source of Christian community: God's love for us in Christ, our being in Christ, and our responsive love toward one another. In Christ, and only in Christ, we discover love for another. But only what is given to us in Christ, not what we can muster, is what is needed for that love.

Genuine love for John now drives away two contaminants of Christian community and peace with God.

#9: LOVE DRIVES AWAY FEAR

Love involves trust. Trust tinged by fear mutes our ability to love someone. It might be fear of their power, fear of their lack of commitment, fear of their volatility, fear of their unreliability, or fear of their unwillingness to love us in return. When our relationship with someone lacks that rugged, affective commitment of presence, advocacy, or direction, fear creeps in that the love will not become an interactive relationship. John takes this into the realm of the divine. When we fear God instead of loving God; when we fear God instead of trusting God, we become aware that we see God as a God of judgment, of anger, of hostility (4:18). Instead, if God is love and if God loves, then we are given every ground for gazing into the face of God in Christ, stepping forward into those divine arms of love, and basking in God's love for us. That location in God's arms drives away all sense of fear.

The tranquility needed for love to flourish cannot coexist with fear of God. Some people have distorted views of God. One study sorted them out as the Authoritative God, the Benevolent God, the Critical God, and the Distant God (Froese and Bader, *America's Four Gods*). However one sorts what people think of God, thinking of God in any other term than "God is love" distorts God. Distorting God diminishes our ability to love God, to know God, and to trust God. Enter fear. John believes love drives fear to the outer limits and beyond (4:18).

#10: LOVE DRIVES
AWAY HATRED

Loving the God who is love, loving the God who resides in us, loving the God who reveals the ultimate love in sending his Son to die for us, and loving the God who has sent the Spirit to us means we enter into an interactive knowing of God called love. Those who love God like this *cannot and choose not to* hate their siblings in Christ. The one who says, "I love God," but "hates one's sibling" is a "falsifier" (4:20; *Second Testament*). These are strong words. Hatred for a sibling in Christ reveals at best a distant relationship with God, if one exists.

The Bible's best Love Chapter, 1 John 4, sketches in bold language a God who is love. This God loves us with the ultimate gift, his Son and the Spirit. This God transforms us through redemption in Christ into agents of divine love in this world. Those who are in Christ find themselves in a family united, not by what we want or know but by God's amazing grace. Maybe family is not the right word. We find ourselves to be lovers—of God, of self, and of one another. Family means lovers. Loving those in that circle with us can become as natural as the love energizing Father, Son, and Spirit in their endless relations of love. Such a love is what genuine knowing is.

What ought to surprise us is that making love this central "makes no sense," which is exactly what Peter Groves writes about here:

> Love makes no sense. It is unsettling, undermining, deconstructive. It turns our world upside down, challenges all our preconceptions, invites us to reconsider the whole of our lives now that love has arrived on the scene. The absurdity of Christianity is not just that the love that makes no sense is the truth that we find in Jesus of Nazareth. The real absurdity of Christianity is the claim that that love is what we are talking about when we are talking about God himself. God is love, and love makes no sense. (Groves, in Strawbridge, et al., *Love Makes No Sense*, 10–11)

QUESTIONS FOR REFLECTION AND APPLICATION

1. What does it mean to say that "God is love"?

2. How do God's love and God's anger relate to each other?

3. How does Jesus reveal God's love?

4. What in your life has impacted your ability to feel or not feel God's love for you?

5. Think of how well you love others in your life, neighbors as well as enemies. How would you rate your love-ability?

FOR FURTHER READING

Dietrich Bonhoeffer, *Life Together* (Minneapolis: Fortress, 1996).

Paul Froese, Christopher Bader, *America's Four Gods: What We Say about God—and What That Says about Us* (updated edition; New York: Oxford University Press, 2015).

Shai Held, *Judaism Is About Love: Recovering the Heart of Jewish Life* (New York: Farrar, Straus and Giroux, 2024).

Again, I recommend highly the study of Patrick Mitchel, *The Message of Love*, The Bible Speaks Today (London: IVP, 2019).

J. I. Packer, *Knowing God* (Downers Grove: IVP, 1993).

Jennifer Strawbridge, Jarred Mercer, Peter Groves, *Loves Makes No Sense: An Invitation to Christian Theology* (London: SCM, 2019).

N. T. Wright, *History and Eschatology: Jesus and the Promise of Eschatology* (Waco: Baylor University Press, 2019).

CENTERING LIFE AROUND JESUS

1 John 5:1–12

¹ Everyone who believes that Jesus is the Christ is born of God, and everyone who loves the father loves his child as well. ² This is how we know that we love the children of God: by loving God and carrying out his commands. ³ In fact, this is love for God: to keep his commands. And his commands are not burdensome, ⁴ for everyone born of God overcomes the world. This is the victory that has overcome the world, even our faith. ⁵ Who is it that overcomes the world? Only the one who believes that Jesus is the Son of God.

⁶ This is the one who came by water and blood—Jesus Christ. He did not come by water only, but by water and blood. And it is the Spirit who testifies, because the Spirit is the truth. ⁷ For there are three that testify: ⁸ the Spirit, the water and the blood; and the three are in agreement. ⁹ We accept human testimony, but God's testimony is greater because it is the testimony of God, which he has given about his Son. ¹⁰ Whoever believes in the Son of God accepts this testimony. Whoever does not believe God has made him out to be a liar, because they have not believed the testimony God has given about his Son. ¹¹ And this is the testimony: God has given us eternal life, and this life is in his Son. ¹² Whoever has the Son has life; whoever does not have the Son of God does not have life.

What goes around in a Celtic knot comes around. That's what we might feel as we read today's passage. I know I did. As with every other passage, repetitions by John do not prevent him from adding a bit here and a bit there. Today's passage centers Jesus, and all the other terms—love, believing, overcoming, commands, testimony—gather around the center of it all: Jesus Christ. The exhortation of 1 John began by centering Jesus in a lyrical set of lines, beginning with "That which was from the beginning, which we have heard, which we have seen with our eyes . . . the Word of life" (1:1). Jesus has been present from 1:1 through chapter four, but chapter five opens with an emphatic recentering of Jesus.

The fundamental question for evangelism in the early church was not so much *Do you want to get saved?* but instead *Who do you think Jesus was?* or *What do you think of Jesus?* The difference between these questions is centering Jesus. So, let's first pull out the strands about Jesus in today's reading.

WHO IS JESUS?

The Bible often reveals who God is, who Jesus is, and who the Spirit is with titles, labels, and adjectives. Thus, in our passage God is the *Father*—new birth happens when someone is "born of God [=Father]" (5:1), which continues in the same verse with "everyone who loves the One who gave life" (*Second Testament*).* By the way, the term "God" often means "Father" in 1 John (e.g., 5:2, 4, 5, 9, 10, 11). The Spirit, often designated as the *Holy* Spirit in the New Testament, in today's reading testifies truth (5:6, 8). Jesus comes to the front stage with labels, adjectives, titles, and actions:

1. Messiah, or Christ (5:1);
2. as God's child, he is to be loved with the Father (5:2, 6);
3. God's Son (5:5, 9, 10, 11, 12);
4. Jesus "came by water and blood" that testify (or witness) to who he is (5:6, 8);
5. God/Father testifies "about his Son" (5:9);
6. in Jesus one is given life, or eternal life (5:11, 12).

The claims the earliest apostles made about Jesus ought to astound us. Our familiarity with our faith, stated as it has been in the Nicene Creed (see p. 64), slows down our perception of how outrageous the claims sounded in the first century. Three observations about our list: First, to be called Messiah means Jesus was anticipated in the promises of the

---

* *The NIV adds "father" with "everyone who loves the father loves his child as well" (5:1). The Greek is not so explicit.*

Bible and he fulfilled those promises, and those promises were all about being the anointed king who would save and govern the people of God. Second, being named God's Son turns a new lens on Jesus that reveals his intimate, eternal relationship with the Father, and that same "Son" language also points to the royalty of the Son, that is, to his kingship and Messiahship. Third, as God's Messiah and Son, Jesus brings redemption, life, and eternal life.

Because these are the truths about Jesus, 1 John in two special passages centers Jesus (1:1–4; 5:1–6). The gospel is about Jesus first before it is about the benefits of salvation. The entirety of 1 John's exhortations to love and to live and to obey are founded on the truths of who Jesus is. The combination of 1 John 1:1–4 and 5:1–6, with the former emphasizing sensory experiences of Jesus and the latter his titles and actions, provided the early church with most of what they needed to believe that Jesus was more than a man, that he was God in the flesh, and that he (as he was eventually described) is the Second Person of the Holy Trinity.

How Do We Know About Jesus?

One of John's favorite terms is translated "testimony," sometimes with "witness," and we meet this term six times in verses nine, ten, and eleven (see 1:2; 4:14; 5:6, 7, 9, 10). A witness is someone who has heard or seen something and verbally states (or declares) what was heard or seen. Such a witness sometimes puts herself in jeopardy for telling the truth. That word "truth" is another element of the theme of witness in 1 John: the witnesses about Jesus are telling God's truth.

Testimony/Witness in 1 John

1 John 1:2 *The life appeared; we have seen it and testify to it, and we proclaim to you the eternal life, which was with the Father and has appeared to us.*

1 John 4:14 *And we have seen and testify that the Father has sent his Son to be the Savior of the world.*

1 John 5:6–7 *This is the one who came by water and blood—Jesus Christ. He did not come by water only, but by water and blood. And it is the Spirit who testifies, because the Spirit is the truth. For there are three that testify . . . .*

1 John 5:9–10 *We accept human testimony, but God's testimony is greater because it is the testimony of God, which he has given about his Son. Whoever believes in the Son of God accepts this testimony. Whoever does not believe God has made him out to be a liar, because they have not believed the testimony God has given about his Son.*

The substance of this witness or testimony includes the facts of Jesus' life, the fact that Jesus is God in the flesh, that he is Messiah, and that he is the Son of God and Savior.

Furthermore, the testimony includes that through Jesus one can be granted the overflowing life that is eternal life (5:6–12; John 10:10).

Jesus and the Spirit are true witnesses (1 John 5:6), but John breaks Jesus' witness into "water and blood" (5:6, 8), and then says these are "God's testimony" (5:9). That expression "water and blood" refers (most likely) to Jesus' baptism and crucifixion, which means the Spirit witnesses to the significance of the saving work of Jesus (cf. 1:9; 2:2; 3:16; 4:14; 5:11). Some think it refers to Jesus' birth (water as amniotic fluid) and death, while others see divine life (water, Spirit) and human life (blood), and this second view once again reminds us that the defectors denied that Jesus had come in the flesh (4:2). That John denies that Jesus came "by water only" sounds like he is responding to someone who claims that water is all one needs. Which suggests, so I think, some were denying the redemptive importance of the cross. God's witness is water and blood, and if a human witness can be accepted for telling the truth, all the more can God's own witness (Spirit, water, blood) be accepted as true (5:9).

Now the point: we know *who Jesus is and what Jesus has accomplished* because of the witness about his baptism and crucifixion, which the Spirit speaks into us, bearing witness with our spirit of the truths of redemption (Romans 8:16). What is remarkable is that John does not appeal to his own witness, as Peter did (cf. 2 Peter 1:16–18). The reliable witness that persuades us of the truth about Jesus comes from the facts of his life (baptism, crucifixion) as communicated to us through the Spirit.

How Do We Respond?

No surprise here: by trusting Jesus and by loving God, which means loving one another. "Everyone who trusts that Yēsous is the Christos has been given life from God." And "everyone who loves the One who gave life loves also the one given life from him" (5:1; *Second Testament*). Yes, that's exactly how the Greek text reads, which the NIV admirably simplifies for us with "everyone who loves the father loves his child" (5:1). This trusting as loving is immediately followed by obeying (5:2–3). This wholehearted and embodied response leads to conquering the world (5:4–5). Again, this network of love flows from the work of God in us.

A truth about the human response to *Who Jesus is* and *What he has done for us* is that faith (or trusting) is a kind of loving, and a loving faith is a kind of obeying, and all this is a kind of knowing and overcoming. That network of terms expresses how our wonderful author, John, does his craft. Love and knowledge and faith and obedience and overcoming interact with one another to form into our response to the Spirit's witness about Jesus.

One single word sums up this network of terms: surrender. Or, if you'd like a close synonym, allegiance. If Jesus is who the Spirit witnesses to us about, the only right response is to give ourselves to Jesus.

What Are the Benefits?

Those who turn to Jesus are "born of God" (5:1), they become agents of love for God, self, and one another (5:1–3), they conquer the world's systems of flesh and pride (5:4–5; cf. 2:16), and they enter into a life that is eternal life (5:11–12). To add others, they experience forgiveness of sins (1:9; 2:2; 3:16; 4:14; 5:11). One word sums this all up: those who respond to Christ enter into *life*, which is yet another of John's favorites (cf. 1:1, 2; 2:25; 3:14, 15; 5:11, 12, 13, 16, 20). This life is being indwelt by God (Father, Son, Spirit) and residing in God (Father, Son, Spirit); it is a new life that overcomes the world's system and embraces a life of love, allegiance to Christ, and the fellowship of love among siblings who also love Christ.

Life in 1 John

1 John 1:1–2 *That which was from the beginning, which we have heard, which we have seen with our eyes, which we have looked at and our hands have touched—this we proclaim concerning the Word of life. The life appeared; we have seen it and testify to it, and we proclaim to you the eternal life, which was with the Father and has appeared to us.*

1 John 2:25 *And this is what he promised us—eternal life.*

1 John 3:14–15 *We know that we have passed from death to life, because we love each other. Anyone who does not love remains in death. Anyone who hates a brother or sister is a murderer, and you know that no murderer has eternal life residing in him.*

138

1 John 5:11–12 *And this is the testimony: God has given us eternal life, and this life is in his Son. Whoever has the Son has life; whoever does not have the Son of God does not have life.*

1 John 5:13 *I write these things to you who believe in the name of the Son of God so that you may know that you have eternal life.*

1 John 5:16 *If you see any brother or sister commit a sin that does not lead to death, you should pray and God will give them life. I refer to those whose sin does not lead to death. There is a sin that leads to death. I am not saying that you should pray about that.*

1 John 5:20 *We know also that the Son of God has come and has given us understanding, so that we may know him who is true. And we are in him who is true by being in his Son Jesus Christ. He is the true God and eternal life.*

Fleming Rutledge reflects on the misadventures we get ourselves into when we "dangle" eternal life in front of people as the motivation for accepting Christ. She once preached these lines: "The idea of believing in Jesus in order to gain eternal life seems somehow repugnant; in the Old Testament, faith in God is the right thing to have just because God is God and there is no way to live a fully human life in this world without him, never mind a life after death which the ancient Hebrews didn't believe in anyway. So it has always seemed to me more than a little manipulative to dangle 'life after death' in front of people in order to convert them" (Rutledge, *The Bible and* The New York Times, 158). John didn't dangle benefits in front of anyone. He presented Jesus to them, and everything flowed from Who he is. With Jesus, they also got life.

The above four points in today's reflection mirror the earliest order of gospeling: it begins with Christ and not with either our problem or what we can gain from the gospel; it centers Jesus Christ—who he is and what he has done; it elevates the necessity of the Spirit's work in us to respond properly; it forms a wholehearted response that is ongoing instead of reducing the response to a single moment; and it then ushers us into the benefits of the gospel, which is a holistic, redemptive experience of life that includes forgiveness, salvation, transformation, glorification, and so much more!

QUESTIONS FOR REFLECTION AND APPLICATION

1. What can we know about Jesus from this passage?

2. How can we know Jesus through the testimony/witness about him?

3. Why is allegiance the right response to learning about Jesus?

4. What is the difference between dangling benefits about Jesus to people versus simply presenting Jesus to them?

5. What might gospeling that centers Jesus sound like?

FOR FURTHER READING

Fleming Rutledge, *The Bible and* The New York Times (Grand Rapids: Wm. B. Eerdmans, 1999).

A LIFE OF CARE
FOR OTHERS

1 John 5:13–21 (reformatted)

¹³ *I write these things to you who believe in the name of the Son of God so that you may know that you have eternal life.* ¹⁴ *This is the confidence we have in approaching God: that if we ask anything according to his will, he hears us.* ¹⁵ *And if we know that he hears us—whatever we ask—we know that we have what we asked of him.*

¹⁶ *If you see any brother or sister commit a sin that does not lead to death, you should pray and God will give them life. I refer to those whose sin does not lead to death. There is a sin that leads to death. I am not saying that you should pray about that.* ¹⁷ *All wrongdoing is sin, and there is sin that does not lead to death.*

¹⁸ <u>*We know*</u> *that anyone born of God does not continue to sin; the One who was born of God keeps them safe, and the evil one cannot harm them.*

¹⁹ *We know that we are children of God, and that the whole world is under the control of the evil one.*

²⁰ *We know also that the Son of God has come and has given us understanding, so that we may know him who is true. And we are in him who is true by being in his Son Jesus Christ. He is the true God and eternal life.*

²¹ *Dear children, keep yourselves from idols.*

Recently a pastor and I wrote a book about those who are undergoing "deconstruction." His name is Tommy Preson Phillips, and our book is called *Invisible Jesus*. (Preson is pronounced "Pree-son.") The subtitle gives our theme away: *A Book about Leaving the Church and Looking for Christ*. Watching social media as we were promoting the book before it was available became an interesting experience. Many seemed to think they knew what we had written and had opinions about the book before they had seen the book itself. A famous line is that "one can't judge a book by its cover" but I would add another: "Don't determine or judge the content of a book until you have read it." The truth is that our book is about caring for those who are struggling with the church. Recently, Kris and I walked by a church sign that said "Feeling disconnected? Try church again." I guffawed at that because of what Tommy and I have learned. For many, the disconnection is actually about the church. Suggesting a return to church is to invite them back into what ails them. "Try Jesus again" would be the improvement we would recommend.

Tommy's and my experience with these deconstructors

unveiled something in a study that we had intuited. Many today think of those who say they are deconstructing as sinners looking to justify their sins, as theological wanderers who no longer believe in orthodoxy, as disaffected Americans who just like to complain. One famous pastor even dismissed deconstruction as sexy. He backed off that dismissal and apologized. But his words spoke what many believe about the deconstructors. We know American Christianity is going through some tough and turbulent times, and we know many are shifting in their faith and allegiances. But what needs to be said, and all this is in chapter two of *Invisible Jesus*, is that the last several years have actually solidified the faith of most of these deconstructors. Such persons are not done with faith, but they may be done with the way a particular church does faith. In some proprietary research a discovery was made that describes the deconstructors and leads us into the final section of 1 John: 86 percent of those who say they are undergoing deconstruction remain in churches. Our book, *Invisible Jesus*, concentrates on that segment of the church. In spite of what pundits on social media and some authors are saying, these deconstructors have not committed a sin that "lead[s] to death" (1 John 5:16). John provides a template for how best to approach those struggling with the church's inconsistencies.

FOR BELIEVERS

As John wrote for believers, so this reflection is for believers. (And *Invisible Jesus* was shaped for leaders in churches and other believers who want to know what's going on and

145

what can be done about it.) John reminds his audience that his exhortation is shaped for those "who believe in the name of the Son of God *so that* [they] may know that [they] have eternal life" (5:13). What are believers to do with those who struggle, who resist, who are wondering if there's a better way to do church, or who can no longer affirm tenets of some church that are not at the center of the Christian faith (like the rapture or six-day creationism or for whom to vote)? John offers four pastoral instructions.

PRAY FOR THEM

Believers can approach God with "frankness" (5:14; *Second Testament*). The NIV's translation "confidence" provides one dimension of this term. Another is that this term was used for those who, when speaking publicly, expressed themselves clearly, boldly, and frankly. The implication of this term is that John wants the believers to ask God for what they want. Instead of a "bless the church" he wants them to ask God in terms like this: "Father, for the sake of your Son give my friend clarity to understand what matters and what does not matter. Give our church leaders the grace to accept that young adults need to individuate in their faith and need space. Prompt the leaders to leave these young adults safe spaces to think about things."

John believes in the God who sees us and hears us. Prayer that is consistent with who God is (as revealed through the Spirit in Jesus) and the ways of God in the past finds resolution prayer time with God (5:14). One of the New Testament's promises, one that many of us stumble over at times, is that if we frankly approach God and ask God for what is consistent with the truth, that God . . . well, John's wording deserves to be heard: "if we know that he hears us about whatever we ask, we know that we have the requests that we have asked from him" (5:15, *Second Testament*). Said more succinctly, God hears us and gives us what we ask.

If we ask God to change the mind of someone wandering into some recent thinking about Paul, we should have no confidence that God will give us what we ask. But, if for the same person we ask God to keep Jesus first and foremost in their thinking, we have every reason to think God will secure that prayer request. We may not see the answer we want now; we may not see the answer as we expected it; but we can be confident that answer will someday arrive. By the time one of these deconstructors comes forward with that very term about themselves, they have been on a journey—sometimes alone, more often with some trusted friends, at times in an online group—for a good while. Their journey may take another two to three years, if not more, before they come to terms with how they see the faith. All this can surround us as we turn to God in prayer for those we care about.

GAIN A NEW PERSPECTIVE

In verses sixteen and seventeen it becomes clear why John began with prayer. The issue is about those who have either sinned or are simply struggling but who have not committed what he calls a sin unto death. We need to delve into what a sin unto death is before we can understand a sin not unto death. All we need to do is take a good look at what John says elsewhere so, first, notice what John says about sin in this exhortation:

1. 1:7–10 teaches that no one is sinless, that Christians sin and are forgiven if they confess.
2. 2:1–12 teaches that true believers follow Jesus, love God, and love one another; that hatred of believers reveals that a person is in the darkness.
3. 3:4–9 teaches that those who continually sin do not know God and are not born of God; those who know God and are born of God do what is right.

John's operating idea is that believers are not sinners and sinners are not believers. But this means his idea of a sinner is one who chooses to walk away from Christ and to live in the flesh, in the world, and in continual sin. These are simple categories; they can make sense of much of life; John is not working with nuances. He is pressing his readers to decide to follow Jesus and to abandon the ways of the world. The best way to do this is with hyperbolic expressions.

With this as the context, a sin unto death describes those who do not believe in Jesus, who walk away from Jesus, and who thus choose the way of the world and its desires and pride (2:16). A sin not unto death then is the occasional, confessed sin of a believer who returns to following Jesus.

For the believer who sins, John instructs believers to pray thus for such a person. Pray that God will give them the life, the eternal life, promised to those who find redemption in

Jesus Christ. John is neither diminishing the reality of sin nor exaggerating his ideas with a demand for sinlessness. As he says it, "All wrongdoing is sin." He knows believers sin. But he also knows "there is a sin that does not lead to death" (5:17). In an almost throwaway two-liner, John also writes, "There is a sin that leads to death. I am not saying that you should pray about that" (5:16). To flip that line, he also does not say you should not pray about that. Or is flipping it misunderstanding him? It's hard for me to think John, the apostle of love, would not pray for those who are wandering from the faith. Perhaps he knows the defectors have gone so far they are no longer capable of repenting. Perhaps, and perhaps not. I speak from experience, both personally and in conversation with others, that most people I know have chosen not to give up on the wandering. What saddens me is that some leaders have so failed to listen to the struggles of others and have hardened their own narrative against the strugglers and now think of them as beyond the pale. This is Christian failure. Who are we to think we know the true state of another person before God?

START WITH POSITIONS OF CONFIDENCE

Three "We knows" appear in verses eighteen through twenty. I reformatted them in the translation above to make these "We knows" stand out. John bolsters confidence in his audience with these three affirmations. The confidence reshapes their prayers for those who are struggling by providing foundations for those prayer requests.

First, he knows believers do not live in sin (5:18a) *because they are preserved* (5:18b). John is unafraid of drawing a line between the world and the people of Jesus, between the flesh and the Spirit, and between believers and unbelievers. He looks out on the streets of Ephesus and observes the lines with utter clarity. And he knows the difference Christ makes is not simply the difference believers make. He knows the difference between believers and unbelievers is *the result of God's redemptive work in the believer through Jesus Christ.* Yet, John is keen on pressing believers to live right.

Now we need to enter into a difficult translation issue. Hang on, and I'll make it as clear as I can. The NIV translates in a way that it is God or Jesus (with its upper case "the One") who "keeps them safe" (5:18b). Yet the Greek is not quite as clear as the NIV's *God keeps them safe.* We begin with the opening: "The One who was born of God." The Greek can be translated with "One" (God) or "one" (the one born again from God). Continuing with verse eighteen, John then writes "keeps himself" or "keeps him/her" or "preserves himself/him." Questions arise: Is it One or one? Who is doing the safekeeping here? Is it him or himself? How do we decide? Context. What precedes that sentence in 5:18b is "the one born of God does not continue" (5:18a) to sin, which undeniably refers to believers. Since the same word is used in the second part, namely, in "the One [or one] who *was born of God*," it is more likely that the second part also refers to a believer, that is, to the one born of God (to "one" and not "One"). To complicate matters, the Greek text has a variant in the last word. Some manuscripts have "him," and others have "himself." If it is the latter, and the latest authoritative text prefers "himself," the term *himself* clearly indicates that it is the "one" and not the "One." If so . . . this is an astounding and important point: the believer, since she has been born of God, is empowered by the indwelling presence of God and responsible to preserve her life by living in faith, love, and obedience.

Second, John knows he and they *are God's children* when the rest of the world has been captured "by the evil one" (5:19). John affirms that believers know who they are: born of God, children of God, indwelt by God. In knowing that, they know their past when they did not know God and when they were in the world. In knowing that they are God's children, they now have come to see the world for its worldliness. Their scope has become cosmic, and their location has become clear. That they know this empowers them to pray for and to restore those who are struggling with faith, love, and obedience. When it comes to the deconstructors of our day, our experience of them has been to recognize the sincere faith of most of them. We do know that some are just hopping off the path and wandering onto other paths. But, through the Spirit, we do discern the presence of God's work in those to whom we have given our listening ears.

Third, he knows God has sent his Son and the *Son's mission is to enlighten the minds of the redeemed* (5:20). The Son's enlightenment, which corresponds to the Spirit's testimony (5:6–12), leads believers to know the truth and to obtain eternal life. We know the Son only because the Son "has given us understanding," and this understanding was given to us— John is walking here in a valuable circle—"So that we may know him who is true." And to go around a circle again in the Celtic knot John creates, because we are "in him who is true" we come to know him who is true! We are "in him [Father God] who is true" because we are "in his Son," and this God is the "true God" and "eternal life" itself! God is not only love. God is life, too.

REMEMBER THE TEMPTATION TO IDOLATRY

A surprising ending. The last line is the only time idolatry is explicitly mentioned in 1 John. So, we take a sweeping view: Ephesus itself was filled with idols and idolatries. From Artemis and her temple, one of the world's greatest achievements of that time, to the pride of the Ephesians and their merchants (Acts 19:23–41), to the goddess Nike's monument on the major street in the city, to shrines in homes, to statues and monuments and altars, the city was filled with reminders of the gods of Rome, of Greece, and of Ephesus. The idols of Rome and Ephesus represented the confluence of both religion and politics. So much so that the worship of the gods was the worship of the people's political leaders. Politics and religion were the same.

Judaism was idol-less and image-less. Jews worshiped a God who is spirit. The God of the Christian faith morphs the God of Judaism into an incarnation of God in Jesus Christ who came in the flesh (4:2). The Christian belief in the invisible God who became visible in Jesus gave to them a double-edged sword against idols and idolatries. Because it did not believe in the gods of Ephesus and because it believed in the invisible

God being incarnate in Jesus, John can doubly warn the believers against falling for the gods of Ephesus. Or, against the subtle power of anything we worship to make us in its image.

Christians today fall for the "God-substitutes" of our world when they don't recognize the seductive power of politics and power (Jobes, *1–3 John*, 245). That is, winning elections, which drives the news cycles about 50 percent of our days, drives the American public so much that presidential candidates and governors of states can become totems of salvation. Victory in an election becomes salvation. It's subtle; it's real; it's all day long in the news cycle. Becoming consciously aware of the seductions of political power, and its cultural barnacles like racism, sexism, and materialism, was the final word of John and it is the final word for us: "keep yourselves from idols," Roman, Ephesian, and American.

QUESTIONS FOR REFLECTION AND APPLICATION

1. What is your perspective on deconstruction and people who deconstruct their faith?

2. How can the Bible help shape our prayers?

3. What is a sin unto death, and how does it differ from a sin not unto death?

4. How do the things we worship make us into their image?

5. In what areas of your life do you need God's enlightenment and redemption?

FOR FURTHER READING

Scot McKnight, Tommy Preson Phillips, *Invisible Jesus: A Book about Leaving the Church and Looking for Christ* (Grand Rapids: Zondervan Reflective, 2024).

2 JOHN

BRIEF
INTRODUCTION
TO 2–3 JOHN

The opening lines of 2 John invite us to introduce some details by way of reminder. The "elder" writes this letter to "the lady chosen by God," or as in *The Second Testament*, "the elect lady-lord" (2 John 1). The vocabulary and style of 2 John evokes 1 John so clearly one has to think they are by the same author, as the church's tradition has always had it. However, the "John" here could be either the apostle John or a slightly younger Elder John. In the second century AD, Papias (quoted later by Eusebius, the first major historian of the church) distinguished the Elder John from the apostle John. Here are his words: "But if someone came who had followed the elders, I made inquiry about the words of the elders, what Andrew or Peter said, or what Philip or what Thomas or James, or what John or Matthias or any other of the Lord's disciples, or what Aristion and the presbyter [elder] John, disciples of the Lord, said" (Eusebius, *Ecclesiastical History* 3.39.4; translation by Schott). In case you wonder if Papias wasn't clear, Eusebius clarifies the words, writing, "Here it is worth recognizing that he counts the name of John twice. The first time he catalogues him with Peter, James, Matthias, and the rest of the apostles, clearly meaning the evangelist [John, the apostle], but by using a distinctive phrase [the presbyter] he ranks the other John with the others outside the number of the apostles, ranking Aristion before him, and clearly naming him a presbyter. This proves the truth of the account of there being two homonymous men in Asia and two tombs in Ephesus, each of which is still said to be John's. And one must apply one's intellect to this. For it is likely that the second John (unless one wishes to claim the first) witnessed the Apocalypse that bears the name of John. The Papias we are now discussing confesses that he received the words of the apostles from those who followed them, but he says that he heard Aristion and the presbyter John with his own ears" (3.39.5).

This much is clear: there were two Johns in Ephesus. One was the apostle, one was the elder. But, is the "elder" of 2 and 3 John the elder alongside Aristion, the one whom Papias himself heard, or is this "elder" the apostle John who wrote the Gospel and 1 John, and for many the book of Revelation? It is not hard for us to read 2 John and connect it to the author of 1 John. Then we read 1 John and connect it reasonably to the Gospel of John. When we proceed like this, we tie all these Johannine books (Gospel, Revelation, 1–3 John) to one and the same author as the history of the tradition has maintained. That is, to the apostle John. However, what clouds the tradition is that 2 and 3 John clearly identify the author as the *Elder*, while 1 John does not. The style of these three letters is so similar we need to think of them as written by the same author. He calls himself the Elder. Is it perhaps the case that the Elder identified himself to distinguish himself from the older apostle? Perhaps so. If so and if the apostle wrote the Gospel of John, the Elder had learned the vocabulary and style of the apostle. An alternative is just as reasonable: the Elder wrote all the Johannine books (Wright and Bird, *The New Testament in Its World*, 652–660, 786–787).

FOR FURTHER READING

N. T. Wright, Michael Bird, *The New Testament in Its World: An Introduction to the History, Literature, and Theology of the First Christians* (Grand Rapids: Zondervan Academic, 2019).

AN ELDER AND
A LADY-LORD

2 John 1–3

¹ The elder,

To the lady chosen by God and to her children,
whom I love in the truth—and not I only, but also all
who know the truth—² because of the truth, which lives
in us and will be with us forever:

³ Grace, mercy and peace from God the Father and
from Jesus Christ, the Father's Son, will be with us in
truth and love.

What is fresh and surprising in 2 John is that the Elder addresses "the lady," the Greek term for whom is *kyria*, the feminine form of "lord." To evoke the connection, I have translated this term as "lady-lord." Now the question of questions for many: Is lady-lord a woman, a woman's name (*Kyria*), or a metaphor for a local church? Since it is very unlikely that the lady-lord and her "children" in verse one are one and the same, it is most likely this lady-lord is not a local church but a woman leader, perhaps named Kyria, of a house church in or around Ephesus, a city teeming with women with positions of influence.* She could be a patroness-pastor much like Lydia (Acts 16:14–15) and Nympha (Colossians 4:15). Thomas Bennett describes the situation well in these words: "We have every reason to believe that wealthy, influential, spiritually mature women could 'mother' believers within John's sphere of influence" (Bennett, *1–3 John*, 111).

The children here are people in the church, and the lady-lord's sister's children are a different local church (2 John 13). The "sister" then could refer to yet another woman leader in an early church in the region around Ephesus.

Truth in John's Letters

1 John 1:6 *If we claim to have fellowship with him and yet walk in the darkness, we lie and do not live out the truth.*

1 John 1:8 *If we claim to be without sin, we deceive ourselves and the truth is not in us.*

1 John 2:4 *Whoever says, "I know him," but does not do what he commands is a liar, and the truth is not in that person.*

---

* *I'm grateful to Sandra Glahn and Lynn Cohick for interacting with me about kyria. Glahn in particular pointed to inscriptions in Ephesus with Artemis Kyria.*

1 John 2:21 *I do not write to you because you do not know the truth, but because you do know it and because no lie comes from the truth.*

1 John 3:18 *Dear children, let us not love with words or speech but with actions and in truth.*

1 John 3:19 *This is how we know that we belong to the truth and how we set our hearts at rest in his presence. . . .*

1 John 4:6 *We are from God, and whoever knows God listens to us; but whoever is not from God does not listen to us. This is how we recognize the Spirit of truth and the spirit of falsehood.*

1 John 5:6 *This is the one who came by water and blood—Jesus Christ. He did not come by water only, but by water and blood. And it is the Spirit who testifies, because the Spirit is the truth.*

2 John 1–2 *The elder, To the lady chosen by God and to her children, whom I love in the truth—and not I only, but also all who know the truth—because of the truth, which lives in us and will be with us forever:*

2 John 3 *Grace, mercy and peace from God the Father and from Jesus Christ, the Father's Son, will be with us in truth and love.*

2 John 4 *It has given me great joy to find some of your children walking in the truth, just as the Father commanded us.*

3 John 1 *The elder, To my dear friend Gaius, whom I love in the truth.*

3 John 3–4 *It gave me great joy when some believers came and testified about your faithfulness to the truth, telling how you continue to walk in it. I have no greater joy than to hear that my children are walking in the truth.*

3 John 8 *We ought therefore to show hospitality to such people so that we may work together for the truth.*

3 John 12 *Demetrius is well spoken of by everyone—and even by the truth itself. We also speak well of him, and you know that our testimony is true.*

Whoever is (or is not) identified as the author of 2 John, the tension over defectors remains (7–11), and that means the message at least reverberates with the message of 1 John. The same major terms appear: truth, love, obedience, deception, and the teaching tradition.

These opening verses emphasize the word "truth." The Elder loves the lady-lord "in the truth." (See Sidebar: Truth in John's Letters.) In fact, all those who "know the truth" love the lady-lord. They love her "because of the truth, which lives in us and will be with us forever" (2). The truth is an all-encompassing sphere in which the believers live and which lives in them. God's redemptive grace, mercy, and peace remain with believers "in truth," which again suggests the sphere in which they live and the faithfulness of God (3). Walking in this truth directs our attention to the content of the gospel as the measure of faithfulness (4). This faithful life, to tap on another important thread in the Celtic knot of terms in these letters, obeys the teachings of Jesus, and that center of his teaching is to love God, to love self, and to love one another. Second John's few verses about truth then correspond with 1 John's verses.

We ought to pause here for a reminder of what truth means in our world: either (1) what is unreachable by humans, leading to relativism or to little more than "my truth" or, when claimed by someone with authority, to personal power claims, or (2) what is scientifically demonstrable. Truth claims in modernity shifted from the truth we know by way of revelation to what we can know and learn from the scientific method. I'm no disbeliever in science or the scientific method. But truth in the context of a fuller sense of life transcends the material and the scientific method. Truth is measured by God and what God reveals in Jesus Christ. Truth for the Christian sense of truth becomes a Person.

The truth is the One Truth, the Lord Jesus Christ, who lives in believers and they in him, and by participating in the One who is Truth, they come to know and love those who are in the circle of truth. Here we find an exhortation to love all those who are in Christ, in spite of differences (and there are many). Love can transcend our capacities to agree, and in many ways the truth and love that unite us turn the voices of difference into the harmony of praise.

QUESTIONS FOR REFLECTION AND APPLICATION

1. Which solution about the identity of the "kyria" makes the most sense of the evidence to you?

2. What is "truth" to John?

3. How do truth and love interweave with each other in these letters?

4. How do love and truth work to create unity among believers?

5. In what ways does the truth of the gospel help you get along with other believers who are different from you?

FOR FURTHER READING

Eusebius, *Ecclesiastical History: A New Translation*, trans. Jeremy M. Schott (Berkeley: University of California, 2019).

THE CELTIC KNOT
OF LOVE

2 John 4–13

⁴ It has given me great joy to find some of your children walking in the truth, just as the Father commanded us. ⁵ And now, dear lady, I am not writing you a new command but one we have had from the beginning. I ask that we love one another. ⁶ And this is love: that we walk in obedience to his commands. As you have heard from the beginning, his command is that you walk in love.

⁷ I say this because many deceivers, who do not acknowledge Jesus Christ as coming in the flesh, have gone out into the world. Any such person is the deceiver and the antichrist. ⁸ Watch out that you do not lose what we have worked for, but that you may be rewarded fully. ⁹ Anyone who runs ahead and does not continue in the teaching of Christ does not have God; whoever continues in the teaching has both the Father and the Son. ¹⁰ If anyone comes to you and does not bring this teaching, do not

take them into your house or welcome them. ¹¹ Anyone
who welcomes them shares in their wicked work.

¹² I have much to write to you, but I do not want to
use paper and ink. Instead, I hope to visit you and talk
with you face to face, so that our joy may be complete.

¹³ The children of your sister, who is chosen by God,
send their greetings.

Genuine pastoral care nurtures the kind of truth that is
indistinguishable from love. As I wrote about 1 John,
one noteworthy Christian thinker has written that "real
knowledge isn't your knowledge of the world or God, but
God's knowledge of you. Your answer to that 'knowledge' is
first and foremost love, because the revelation is itself love"
(N. T. Wright, *History and Eschatology*, 207). Since all knowing is relational, only the deepest of relations, love, knows
fully. Knowing, truth, and love form a Celtic knot in the
Elder's teaching, and it is the knot into which we all need to
enter. If we separate what God unites, we cut the knot. The
beauty of the knot is then defaced.

Karen Jobes reveals that many today have cut that knot.
Here's how she says it: "In our modern way of thinking truth
is cognitive while love is emotional, and the two are not nec-
essarily related." (While actually, emotion is cognitive as well
as affective.) She is right about that cutting of the knotting of
love and truth in the Bible. She continues with this piercing
reminder: "They are so closely related that they are essentially
concomitant; one cannot love genuinely apart from the truth,

and one does not know truth truly until one loves (1 John 3:18; 5:2)" (Jobes, *1–3 John*, 258). God's love reveals true love: God's love is a rugged, affective commitment to be with us (presence) and for us (advocacy) that transforms us into those who grow in loving a relational, interactive God as God loves (direction). That direction, according to our fourth element, is Christlike and transforms us into Christlikeness in our love. And our love looks like God's love: our love is a rugged, affective commitment to be with a person (presence) and to be for a person (advocacy) in order for both lover and beloved to grow together in virtue (direction), or Christlikeness or Christoformity.

TRUTH, LOVE, OBEDIENCE

The knot of love, truth, and obedience is old yet new, and when the Elder observes or hears that (at least some of) the children of this lady-lord are walking in the truth-that-is-love, he is full of "joy" (4). Walking in love is old because it is from the Father, which evokes the Shema of Deuteronomy 6:4–9, and it is new because Jesus summed up the Father's will for us with the Jesus Creed of loving God, self, and our neighbors (Mark 12:28–34; cf. John 13:34–35). From the beginning the lady-lord learned this as the basic Christian way of life (2 John 5).

"This is love: that we walk in obedience to his commands" (6). Following this knot leads under (or is it over?) other lines. Truth, love, and obedience are knotted together. For many of us, contending that love is a command, or an order, strains our senses because we want love to be deeper, an instinct, an emotion. It is deeper, and the truth is in us, and that truth is the gospel about Jesus, and the gospel of Jesus generates a life of love that looks like the life of Jesus. These themes, too, are part of the knot. The knot is unbroken; there are not three, four, or five threads in this knot. The one thread in this knot is all of these at the same time, looping around and inside and over other lines.

Is the knot love, with all the other favorite terms of John the threads?

DECEPTION AND TEACHING

This Elder worries about children being deceived. Some in Ephesus were denying what the Elder knew was true: Jesus is Israel's long-expected Messiah (1 John 2:22); Jesus is God come-in-the-flesh (4:2); and Jesus is the one true source of life (5:11–13). Those who deny these truths are driven by anti-christ, and at the heart of antichrist is to deny that "Jesus Christ [has come] in the flesh" (2 John 7). What the Elder says in verse eight with "Watch out that you do not lose" echoes the idea we find in Revelation 2:4 as what did happen in Ephesus: they lost their first love. That the Elder uses "reward" in 2 John 7 also echoes Revelation 2:7's promise of a reward. Furthermore, the deceivers of Revelation 2:2 find a presence in 2 John 7–11.

The problem of deception is easier to believe in than to detect. What one person thinks is deception, another person thinks is a radical commitment or a biblical teaching.

One could think of the dangers of capitalism, of racist church structures and systems, of sexist power plays and abuses in the church, and of political idolatries, whether to the left or to the right. Here is one example that my son pointed out to me some years ago. As a professional baseball scout, he had become attuned to how we speak of those from other races. I will let the Cuban Miguel Echevarría restate what I learned from my son: "Latinos/as in ecclesial settings, for example, are sometimes complimented on how well we speak English or how intelligent we are. While these remarks seem innocent enough, they communicate people's biases: they don't expect Latinos or Latinas to speak good English or to be intelligent" (Echevarría, "1–3 John," 724). When these sorts of falsehoods pervade the church so that we don't even notice the condescensions, we are in danger of walking away from the gospel. We are being captured by a deception, a deception connected to antichrist, when we indwell racist systems.

Let's also think of the prosperity gospel of so many today. That is, that faithfulness inevitably leads to both material blessings and health and healing. If we are not experiencing both, our faith has diminished. One can point to the famous Magna Carta for this theology in Deuteronomy 28, or to Jesus' healings and to his promise that our prayers will be answered, which John echoes in 1 John 5:15. It's not that there isn't some biblical anchor for believing in human flourishing. The problem arises when that is the only anchor, or that becomes the dominating anchor. A boat with one anchor spins in the winds and waves. The deception occurs when human flourishing denies the reality of pain, suffering, and even death. So many deceptive ideas in the Christian marketplace are distortions of truths and magnifications of a single verse or passage in ways that silence or even deny other passages. (An online link to a discussion of prosperity theology can be found in For Further Reading.)

Let us also remind ourselves that scouts for deception can be seriously misguided as well. We sometimes refer to some of them today as "watch blogs," and at times they can set themselves as always right—*but only because they have formed the skill of pointing out the errors of others!* Thomas Slater warns us of the danger of thinking we are right, others are wrong, and that denouncing others may cast out genuine believers: "Christian history is fraught with ethno-religious conflicts that have magnified beyond control: the Catholic-Protestant conflict in Northern Ireland, the Catholic-Muslim-Orthodox strife in the former Yugoslavia, to name a few. No side is absolutely correct, and none is absolutely incorrect. All sinfully act as if they are without error" (Slater, "1–3 John," 542). I'm grateful for Slater's expression: "All sinfully act as if they are without error." Let us exercise caution in denouncing others who claim the faith; let us be discerning as well. Let us be humble about our discernments.

The Elder casts an image for all of us to appropriate: "Anyone who runs ahead and does not continue in the teaching of Christ does not have God" (2 John 9). The idea is someone going ahead or even extending the teachings of Jesus beyond consistency with Jesus. John saw others as having entered into the danger zone of abandoning the truth and becoming a captive of the antichrist. While we are always called to discern how to walk on the path of Jesus, there is plenty of terrain where Jesus has not been. What matters is that the path we cut consistently lines up with the path Jesus carved out for us, and that path was the path of loving God, loving self, and loving others. Which sounds like we can do or say and teach anything we want if we love. Emphasizing love can also be a problem. We ought to remember that one who cared deeply about theological truths, St. Augustine, once said this about the mistaken readings of the Bible, that if they end up at the location that builds up love (or charity) they are helpful interpretations:

> So if it seems to you that you have understood the divine scriptures, or any part of them, in such a way that by this understanding you do not build up this twin love of God and neighbor, then you have not yet understood them. If on the other hand you have made judgments about them that are helpful for building up this love, but for all that have not said what the author you have been reading actually meant in that place, then your mistake is not pernicious. . . .
>
> But any who understand a passage in the scriptures to mean something which the writer did not mean are mistaken, though the scriptures are not deceiving them. But all the same, as I had started to say, if they are mistaken in a judgment which is intended to build up charity, which is *the end of the law* (1 Timothy 1:5), they are mistaken in the same sort of way as people who go astray off the road, but still proceed by rough paths to the same place as the

road was taking them to. Still, they must be put right, and shown how much more useful it is not to leave the road, in case they get into the habit of deviating from it, and are eventually driven to take the wrong direction altogether. (Augustine, *Teaching Christianity*, p. 129; 1.36.40–41)

Yet, as Augustine also taught throughout his entire career in the church, the love of God that Jesus teaches is a love that affirms the truth about God, the truth of the gospel, the truth about who Jesus is, the truth about the world and the flesh and the pride of life, and a life of fellowship with fellow lovers of Jesus.

The Elder warns then with strong words. Hospitality was a highly ranked virtue in earliest Christianity. Yet hospitality was also sacred. The Elder insists that the children of the lady-lord not offer hospitality to the deceivers. Deceivers are those who deny the teachings about Jesus and of Christ (9–10), and the Elder warns them that offering Christian hospitality, which is spiritual fellowship and mutual growing in Christ together, to deceivers locates these children in the "wicked work" of the falsifiers of truth (10–11).

Instead of writing, the Elder would rather be "face to face," which literally reads "mouth to mouth" (12; *Second Testament*). I like email, and I like Facebook Messenger, and I can use the DM of X, and I at times use Threads, but the best form of communication is person to person, face to face. Conversations on a walk or sitting down over coffee or in a living room, or over the phone and on Zoom, are the purest forms, while all indirect communications (email, etc.) are but imitations of person-to-person communication. There are times for indirect conversation because they can get things down in ways that verbal communication might not accomplish. But there are times for direct conversations because in such a setting we can read the face, hear the tone, and know the deeper intent of those with whom we speak. I do hundreds of podcasts a year, and 99 percent of them are both audio and video. We do video so we can read the faces of those to whom we are speaking, yet my calculation is that 99 percent of the podcasts are broadcasted only in audio. The Elder's version of "mouth to mouth" remains a vital reminder of the importance to embodied presence with others.

Letters often end with customary greetings from those in the author's presence. The Elder's is "the children of your sister," and I think this is most likely a genuine sibling of the lady-lord, who [also] is "chosen by God, send their greetings." If the Elder is in Ephesus, one can surmise the lady-lord is probably in the circuit of churches to which John sent the Apocalypse. That is, Smyrna, Pergamum, Thyatira, Sardis, Philadelphia, or Laodicea.

QUESTIONS FOR REFLECTION AND APPLICATION

1. How does love transform us into Christlikeness?

2. Look up Deuteronomy 6:4–9 and Mark 12:28–34. What does the "Jesus Creed" teach us about the basic Christian way of life?

3. How do all of John's favorite terms work together as threads to form a knot of love?

4. What are some of the benefits and pitfalls of discerning deceptions in the church?

5. Imagine John could deliver the message of these letters to you "face to face" (or "mouth to mouth"). How would that impact your reception of these messages?

FOR FURTHER READING

Saint Augustine, *Teaching Christianity: De Doctrina Christiana* (trans. Edmund Hill; New York: New City Press, n.d.).

N. T. Wright, *History and Eschatology: Jesus and the Promise of Eschatology* (Waco: Baylor University Press, 2019).

To learn more about Prosperity Theology: https://en.wikipedia.org/wiki/Prosperity_theology.

3 JOHN

LOVING A CHILD
IN THE FAITH

3 John 1–4

¹ The elder,

> *To my dear friend Gaius, whom I love in the truth.*
>
> *² Dear friend, I pray that you may enjoy good health and that all may go well with you, even as your soul is getting along well. ³ It gave me great joy when some believers came and testified about your faithfulness to the truth, telling how you continue to walk in it. ⁴ I have no greater joy than to hear that my children are walking in the truth.*

Early church ministry, like today, involved specific people. In 3 John we encounter three names: the letter recipient Gaius (1), the divisive Diotrephes (9), and the letter carrier Demetrius (12). The "elder" (1) has been traditionally connected to the apostle John, but there were two Johns in Ephesus. One was the apostle, one was the elder. But is the "elder" of 2 and 3 John the elder John or the apostle John? It is not hard for us to read 2 John and connect it to the author of 1 John. As we stated in the Introduction and in the Brief Introduction to 2 and 3 John, there are reasons to think all these books were written by the Elder John, not John, son of Zebedee, and apostle.

The Elder informs us that Gaius is someone he loves in the truth (see pp. 162–164 Sidebar on Truth, comments on 2 John 1–3), and it appears that Gaius is one of the Elder's converts, or at least one of his congregants: he is one of his "children" (4). Recall that love and truth, with its needed idea of knowing, are knotted in these letters. Notice, too, that the Elder has a loving, parental relationship with Gaius, who was probably the host of a house church as he was capable of offering hospitality to "foreigners" or perhaps visiting believers from other locations (5–8), and it is clear the Elder plans to partake in Gaius's hospitality in the future (13–14). Demetrius is expected to be shown hospitality when this letter arrives (12). Gaius is respected by those who have arrived in Ephesus (3).

That the Elder loves Gaius comes to expression in "Dear friend" (3 John 2), which could be translated "Loved one" (*Second Testament*). It is a bit short-sighted to see the relationship of the Elder and Gaius to be one of friendship. The relationship is familial, that is, it is a relationship of a parent/father to a child/son in the faith. Yes, friendship captures some of this relationship, but friends and family were then and today substantively different relationships. We could speculate that Gaius may have been through a rough patch health-wise because of the Elder's wishes for his health (2), but it is more likely that the Elder opens this personal letter with commonplace wishes for health. The expression that "all may go well with you" more literally, and more picturesquely, reads "I formulate a prayer for you to make a good path" (*Second Testament*). Which reminds us of the Irish prayer one at times sees at doors as one is leaving:

> *May the road rise up to meet you.*
> *May the wind be always at your back.*
> *May the sun shine warm upon your face,*
> *the rains fall soft upon your fields,*
> *and until we meet again, may God hold you in the palm*
> *of His hand.**

These blessings for physical well-being lead to "just as your self is on a good path." The NIV turns it into a commonplace with "even as your soul is getting along well." The term behind *The Second Testament*'s "self" and the NIV's "soul" is *psyche*, a term that names a person's being, life, and soul. Too often "soul" has been assigned to the immaterial, to the inner person, and even to some immortal soul, but such ideas derive from Greek philosophers, like Plato, more than the Jewish world. The term refers to a whole person's life and self.

Wherever the Elder is, and I think he's in Ephesus, some "brothers" (*Second Testament*; NIV has "believers") had arrived in Ephesus from Gaius's location, "witnessing your Truth . . . just as you walk around in Truth" (3; *Second Testament*). I find

---

* *(https://www.theirishroadtrip.com): one can find this anywhere online.*

it unnecessary for the NIV to turn this important term in these letters (truth) into "faithfulness to the truth." As we discovered in 2 John, believers live in the truth and remain with us (2 John 2, 4). Gaius is one of whom the Elder approves, which means Gaius flourishes because he walks around in the truth.

Gaius or Gaiuses in the New Testament?

Because the name Gaius was so common we can easily think of three or four named Gaiuses in the New Testament: one in Macedonia, one in Derbe, one in Corinth, and one in Asia (3 John). Yet, because travel was common and because of the distance between the locations of a Gaius in these texts, it is entirely possible for the Gaius of 3 John to be the Gaius of these other texts. One reasonably clear indicator that the Gaius connected to the Pauline churches is not the Gaius of 3 John is that the Elder calls Gaius one of his children. That probably indicates the Elder participated in his conversion and baptism. One early Christian tradition states that John placed Gaius as bishop in Pergamum (cf. Acts 20:4).

Acts 19:29 *[In Ephesus] Soon the whole city was in an uproar. The people seized Gaius and Aristarchus, Paul's traveling companions from Macedonia, and all of them rushed into the theater together.*

Acts 20:4 *He was accompanied by Sopater son of Pyrrhus from Berea, Aristarchus and Secundus from Thessalonica, Gaius from Derbe, Timothy also, and Tychicus and Trophimus from the province of Asia.*

Romans 16:23 *[In Cenchraea or Corinth] Gaius, whose hospitality I and the whole church here enjoy, sends you his greetings. Erastus, who is the city's director of public works, and our brother Quartus send you their greetings.*

1 Corinthians 1:14 *I thank God that I did not baptize any of you except Crispus and Gaius . . . .*

QUESTIONS FOR REFLECTION AND APPLICATION

1. Which theory about the author of these letters makes the best sense of the evidence to you?

2. How is John the Elder's relationship with Gaius a good example of how John sees his converts/congregants as "children"?

3. Who do you think this Gaius might be?

4. In what ways do you see your relationships with other Christians as family relationships?

5. Think of people for whom you have played a spiritually shaping role. Do you think of them as your spiritual children? Why or why not?

HOSPITALITY
AND TRIBALISM

3 John 5–10

[5] *Dear friend, you are faithful in what you are doing for the brothers and sisters, even though they are strangers to you.* [6] *They have told the church about your love. Please send them on their way in a manner that honors God.* [7] *It was for the sake of the Name that they went out, receiving no help from the pagans.* [8] *We ought therefore to show hospitality to such people so that we may work together for the truth.*

[9] *I wrote to the church, but Diotrephes, who loves to be first, will not welcome us.* [10] *So when I come, I will call attention to what he is doing, spreading malicious nonsense about us. Not satisfied with that, he even refuses to welcome other believers. He also stops those who want to do so and puts them out of the church.*

Hospitality, an expression of Christian love and generosity, was at the heart of Christian travel in the early centuries of our faith. Travel was taxing and could become expensive. It was often dangerous. As churches began to pop up in the cities left behind in the Pauline and Johannine missions (see the end comment on 2 John 4–13), Christian travelers depended on the hospitality of believers. Hospitality was more than cookies and coffee in the fellowship hall, though such moments in our churches are forms of Christian hospitality. Hospitality was bed and breakfast and lunch and dinner, depending on how you name meals, but also fellowship in the Spirit and worship and instruction and education. Christian hospitality became a medium for news about other churches, for experiencing diversity among the churches, and an opportunity to pass on news to others as one sent off the one who temporarily stayed in a home. Third John 9 assumes the common practice of Christian letters of affirmation, which the traveler presented to places of hospitality. In the world of this letter Christian hospitality can be connected to Jewish, Greek, and Roman temple hospitality. In the latter, the temple and its authorities provided hospitality for those who arrived in order to worship or participate in a sacrificial event. At least one synagogue in Jerusalem had guest rooms for visitors.

HOSPITALITY AFFIRMED

The Elder commends and honors Gaius for being faithful in his etiquette of hospitality. His actions expressed allegiance to Christ and to Christians in need of bed and board, and they could be "foreigners." The Greek term is *xenos*, which can denote strangers, outsiders, and foreigners. The term for hospitality is *philoxenia*, but it is not found in the letters of John. Hospitality is clear in today's reading in these terms: "in what you are doing," in "strangers," in "please send them on their way," in "they went out" to further the mission, in "receiving no help from the pagans," and in "we are obligated to take up such persons" (8; *Second Testament*; NIV has "show hospitality"). Second John had some sharp terms about not offering hospitality (2 John 10–11). Ironically, a man named Diotrephes apparently refused to offer hospitality to the Elder or to others connected to the Elder (3 John).

Those to whom Gaius offered hospitality informed "the church" about Gaius's "love" (6), which here indicates (again) hospitality. An element of the etiquette of hospitality is to provide the traveler with provisions when they move on. The Elder instructs Gaius to be generous (6) and compares this form of gracious generosity to the "ethnic groups" (7; *Second Testament*) who don't offer hospitality. The NIV's "pagans" unnecessarily limits the meaning of the term to idolatries and religious practices. In fact, "pagans" disconnects us from a valuable connection we need today, while "ethnic groups" connects us to a glaring issue: the lack of hospitality white American Christianity offers to those who come from Latin American, African American, and Asian American ethnic groups (Echevarría, "1–3 John," 726). Thomas Slater refers to this as the unfortunate habit of multiplying churches by dividing by ethnic groups (Slater, "1–3 John," 542). Hospitality, the Elder reminds Gaius, forms into the network of mutual support for the gospel (8).

Tribalism Denounced

A problem arose in that same "church" mentioned in verse six. A certain Diotrephes has made it clear he will not welcome or offer hospitality to the Elder (9). Diotrephes gets a brilliant first-century description of a narcissist: "who loves first place for himself" (9; *Second Testament*). Put directly, Diotrephes rejects the leadership of the Elder. If he welcomes those sent by the Elder, he admits the leadership of the Elder. Narcissists view the world through the lens of who can build up and affirm the narcissist's status, honor, and glory. They have detectors for those who will not fall in line, and it leads them to forms of tribalism: those who are "with them" and those who are "against them." One habit of the narcissistic leader is to degrade others through gossip, innuendo, labeling, urging others to dissociate with their rivals, wanting the rivals to leave, and expressing relief and a sense of unity when the group gets rid of those who call out the abuses. The Elder speaks here of "spreading malicious nonsense about us" (10). The criticisms more often than not are less about accuracy than forming and maintaining one's tribe.

Diotrephes fits this description because he—and here I translate woodenly to evoke the Elder's way with words— does not "recognize the siblings," which refers to turning them away at the door (10). Furthermore, he "prohibits those wanting," and the Elder does not complete what they want, but it's clear enough: he puts a stop to those who do want to recognize and open the door to the siblings in Christ who are in need of hospitality. What's worse is that he "tosses them from the assembly" (*Second Testament*) if they do welcome the travelers! For this narcissist the only ones who can be accepted in the fellowship are those who agree with him and who will do what he wants them to do.

What caused this problem? Karen Jobes discusses the options, and my summary of her discussion follows:

1. Diotrephes did not accept the authority and leadership of the Elder;
2. they differed significantly in theology;
3. they had an interpersonal clash;
4. Diotrephes, worried about heresies, prohibited traveling teachers in his community;
5. a mix of some or all of the above! (Jobes, *1–3 John*, 316–319)

Diotrephes had enough power or authority to ban hospitality for some and to prohibit locals to offer hospitality to those whom he had banned. Authority and power are at least involved. If we connect the problems at work in 1 and 2 John to Diotrephes, we could claim the problem was theological. That would suggest the man had a low Christology and stood with those who denied Jesus had come in the flesh (1 John 4:2; 2 John 7). But the Elder does not pin either of the issues in #1 or #2 when he describes Diotrephes. All he tells us is that Diotrephes banned hospitality for some. It is wisest to admit we can't be reasonably sure but that probably #3 or #4, or a mix of them, come closest to what we can know.

QUESTIONS FOR REFLECTION
AND APPLICATION

1. How are hospitality in the early church and hospitality in the church today different and similar?

2. What can multiethnic churches illustrate about Christian hospitality?

3. Compare and contrast what the Elder writes about Gaius and Diotrephes. Thomas Bennett writes, "In everything John praises Gaius, he swiftly condemns its opposite in Diotrephes." Do you see this, too?

4. How can narcissism impede hospitality?

5. What hospitable practices would you like to increase in your life?

BASIC CHRISTIAN PRINCIPLES

3 John 11–15

[11] Dear friend, do not imitate what is evil but what is good. Anyone who does what is good is from God. Anyone who does what is evil has not seen God. [12] Demetrius is well spoken of by everyone—and even by the truth itself. We also speak well of him, and you know that our testimony is true.

[13] I have much to write you, but I do not want to do so with pen and ink.

[14] I hope to see you soon, and we will talk face to face.

[15] Peace to you. The friends here send their greetings. Greet the friends there by name.

If we transport ourselves to the first century where believers were a tiny minority held in contempt by some, suspicion by many, and simply weird by nearly everyone, we will understand the care taken by Christians when they chose to offer hospitality to someone knocking on the door. A basic Christian principle was to "imitate" what is good and not what is evil, and that good people do good things and bad people do bad things. Those doing evil have "not seen God" (11). These words echo Jesus' words in Matthew 7:15–20. In this context, doing good means offering hospitality to those sent by the Elder because hospitality expresses solidarity in the community of Jesus, adherence to the belief that Christ has come in the flesh.

The Elder in this final paragraph mentions yet one more name, Demetrius, who was both in need of hospitality and carried the letter from the Elder to the church where Diotrephes stirred up dissension. He is thus one of those to whom Diotrephes refused hospitality (10). The Elder affirms Demetrius in this letter to vouchsafe for him. The Elder describes Demetrius as one who is "well spoken of by everyone," so much so it can be said he was affirmed "by truth itself" (12)! To ramp up this affirmation of Demetrius the Elder connects the man not only to truth, but the Elder's own words to truth: "our testimony is true" (12).

As was the case with 2 John 12, so in verse 13–14 here: the Elder prefers face-to-face communication to writing. He has so much to say that he wants to wait for that setting. Kris and I did this very thing today when we were walking. A close friend of ours texted us about something. We discussed it but knew texting could lead to too many thumb-mistakes and too much of a back-and-forth. So we called, turned the iPhone to speaker, and had a thirty-two-minute conversation, which ended just as we entered our home at the end of our walk. Talking is better than texting, and sitting down with someone is even better than talking on the phone.

I like the ending of this letter. "Peace to you" may be the boilerplate Jewish blessing (*shalom*), but boilerplate does not diminish the tradition and meaning of that term. It evokes living in the world as God made the world to be lived in, as it also evokes blessing Gaius. Notice that "to you" is singular, but the Elder then turns to others, both those with him—their "friends" with him greet Gaius—and all their friends there, whom the Elder urges Gaius to greet. His interpersonal skills rise to the top. As he wanted to talk face to face, so he wants Gaius to greet the Elder's friends there "by name" (15).

QUESTIONS FOR REFLECTION AND APPLICATION

1. In what ways are Christians considered "weird" today?

2. What does the Elder say in affirmation of Demetrius?

3. How does goodness in our lives identify us with God?

4. Does the truth, and do other believers, speak well of you?

5. If you could speak face to face with Elder John after reading these letters, what would you like to say to him in response?

Also Available in the
New Testament Everyday Series

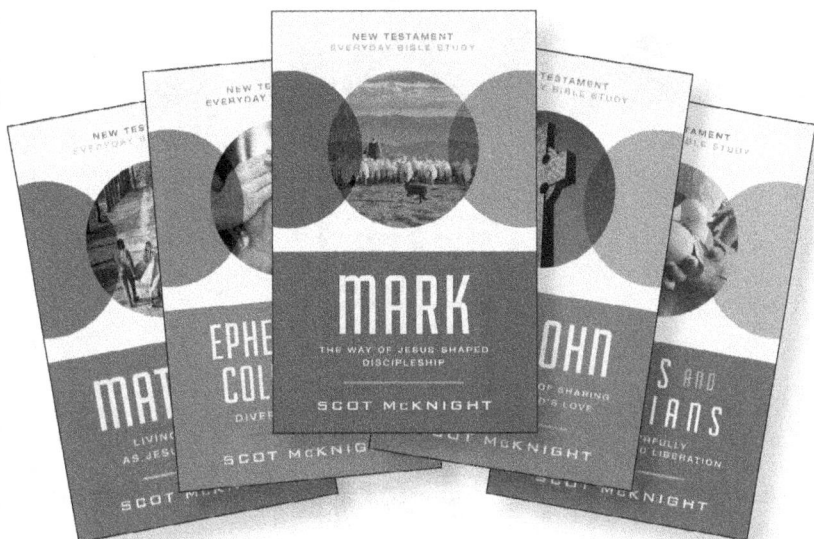

The Blue Parakeet, 2nd Edition

Rethinking How You Read the Bible

Scot McKnight, author of The Jesus Creed

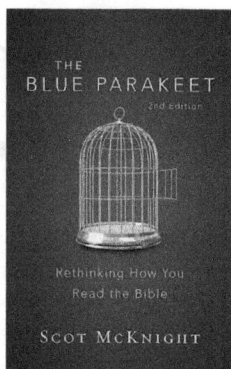

How are we to live out the Bible today? In this updated edition of *The Blue Parakeet*, you'll be challenged to see how Scripture transcends culture and time, and you'll learn how to come to God's Word with a fresh heart and mind.

The gospel is designed to be relevant in every culture, in every age, in every language. It's fully capable of this, and, as we read Scripture, we are called to discern how God is speaking to us today.

And yet applying its words and directions on how to live our lives is not as easy as it seems. As we talk to the Christians around us about issues that matter, many of us wonder: how on earth are we reading the same Bible? How is it that two of us can sit down with the same Bible and come away with two entirely different answers about everything from charismatic gifts to the ordaining of women?

Professor and author of *The King Jesus Gospel* Scot McKnight challenges us to rethink how to read the Bible, not just to puzzle it together into some systematic belief or historical tradition but to see it as an ongoing Story that we're summoned to enter and to carry forward in our day.

What we need is a fresh blowing of God's Spirit on our culture, in our day, and in our ways. We need twenty-first-century Christians living out the biblical gospel in twenty-first-century ways. And if we read the Bible properly, we will see that God never asked one generation to step back in time and live in ways of the past.

Through the Bible, God speaks in each generation, in that generation's ways and beckons us to be a part of his amazing story.

Available in stores and online!

ZONDERVAN®

Following King Jesus

We want to follow King Jesus, but do we
know how?

Author and professor Scot McKnight will
help you discover what it means to follow
King Jesus through 24 lessons based on four
of his writings (*The King Jesus Gospel*, *The
Blue Parakeet - 2nd edition*, *One.Life*, and *A
Fellowship of Differents*). McKnight's unique
framework for discipleship is designed to be
used for personal study and within disciple-
making groups of two or more. In this workbook, McKnight will help you:

Study Guide
9780310105992

- Know the biblical meaning of the gospel
- Read the Bible and understand how to
  apply it today
- Live as disciples of Jesus in all areas of life
- Show the world God's character through life together in the church

Each lesson, created by Becky Castle Miller, has both Personal Study
and Group Discussion sections. The Personal Study section contains a
discipleship reading from Scot McKnight, an insightful Bible study, an insightful Bible study, and a time for individual prayer, action, and reflection.
The Group Discussion section includes discussion questions and activities
to do together with a discipleship group. You'll share insights from your
personal study time with each other and explore different ways of living
out what you're learning.

Whether you have been a Christian for many years or you are desiring
a fresh look at what it means to be a disciple, this workbook is an in-depth
guide to what it means to follow King Jesus and to discover how to put that
kind of life into practice.

Harper*Christian*
Resources